liß schreibe ich zu ihmer ehereuder
zeitzniß zu Lunden den 23 april
anno 16 16
Bernhardt Wilhelm von Maßbach

James I of Great Britain

op sulcken karen word Het go
London over Straet gebract

Lot

Een Porterofte
Arbeÿder van londor

CONTENTS

SHAKESPEARE
COURT, CROWD AND PLAYHOUSE

François Laroque

THAMES AND HUDSON

Shakespeare is a universal genius. His works are now read and performed everywhere. Yet he started life as the son of a Stratford glover, given a no more than average education, but intensely curious about the world around him. Town scenes, country customs and superstitions, the fairs and popular entertainments of his childhood, were his raw material as much as tales of kings and noblemen.

CHAPTER 1
STRATFORD-UPON-AVON

The theatre was a popular form of entertainment in the 16th century, as seen in this painting of a village fair (left) by Dutch artist David Vinckboons. Strolling players (right) visited all small towns.

It was to Stratford that a certain John Shakespeare came in about 1550, from the nearby village of Snitterfield, where his father Richard Shakespeare was a prosperous farmer. He set up in business as a glove-maker and also traded profitably in wool and meat. In 1557 he married Mary Arden, the youngest of eight daughters of Robert Arden of Wilmcote, a little hamlet near Snitterfield. The Ardens were a rich family in the county of Warwickshire; and Arden was also the name of a forest outside Stratford, later to feature in Shakespeare's pastoral comedy *As You Like It*, written in about 1599.

Stratford-upon-Avon was a tranquil market town lying in a lovely wooded valley and famous for its fairs. London was two days away on horseback or four days on foot, and the great Midland towns, Worcester, Warwick and Oxford, were within striking distance.

Map of England in 1579, Stratford at its heart. 'This royal throne of kings, this scepter'd isle,/ This earth of majesty, this seat of Mars,/ This other Eden, demi-paradise'(*Richard II*, Act II.i).

Stratford's strategic position at a crossroads is suggested by the etymology of its name, signifying a 'ford by which a Roman road crossed the river'. A fief of the bishops of Worcester in the Middle Ages, the

John Shakespeare's business premises were in the west wing of his house in Henley Street, which, as far back as one can trace, was

town had by the end of the 12th century acquired a degree of autonomy. Two fine churches of 13th-century origin survive: the parish church of the Holy Trinity and the Guild Chapel. The Guild built the grammar school, formally re-established by Edward VI as the King's New School. Also in Stratford is the handsome stone bridge first constructed in 1490 by Sir Hugh Clopton, a local luminary who had made his fortune in London and built New Place, the mansion later bought by William Shakespeare. John Shakespeare prospered in Stratford. In 1556 he bought two houses, one of them in Henley Street, where he had been living since 1552.

known as the 'woolshop' – evidence that he traded in wool, and possibly skins, in addition to working as a glover. This contemporary engraving shows a craftsman making gloves and leather purses. True to his origins, Shakespeare did not forget the traditions of the craft in his plays, in which he made frequent use of glove imagery. The clown Feste, for example, gives this definition of wit: 'A sentence is but a chev'ril glove to a good wit. How quickly the wrong side may be turn'd outward' (*Twelfth Night*, Act III.i).

Soon afterwards he entered public life. He joined the council in 1557, becoming alderman in 1565, then bailiff in 1568. The following year he unsuccessfully applied to the College of

Heralds for a grant of arms. And here his social ascent was brought to an abrupt end. In 1577, burdened by heavy fines and increasing debt, he was obliged to mortgage his wife's property. For reasons that remain mysterious he ceased to attend the meetings of the council, which expelled him in 1586. He also stopped going to church, no doubt from fear of running into his creditors.

Early years

Against the date 26 April 1564, the Stratford parish register records the baptism of: '*Gulielmus filius Johannes Shakspere*' (William, son of John Shakespeare). Born in a little house in Henley Street, William was the first son of John and Mary Shakespeare, the third of their eight children. His birthday is, appropriately, celebrated on 23 April, the feast of St George, patron saint of England.

The boy William attended the local school at Stratford. From the age of four or five children were taught to read, write and count by a master known as

The naive lack of proportion apparent in this engraving of an Elizabethan school suggests the awe in which the redoubtable 'abecedarius' was held.

an 'abecedarius'. They recited the alphabet using an ABC, or horn-book, and did their reading practice on the catechism. They were introduced to Latin by means of *Lily's Grammar* and set to learn Latin

Shakespeare makes fun of schoolmasters in his comedies, as in this extract from the absurd Latin lesson given by Sir Hugh Evans to the boy William Page.
'EVANS: What is "lapis", William?

maxims by heart. In his plays Shakespeare often presents schoolmasters in a somewhat ridiculous light, as for example the pedantic Holofernes in *Love's Labour's Lost* or the parson Sir Hugh Evans, who gives a memorable and obscene Latin lesson in *The Merry Wives of Windsor* (Act IV.i.). Shakespeare also harks back to his school days in *As You Like It* (Act II.vii.), with Jaques'

WILLIAM: A stone.
EVANS: And what is "a stone", William?
WILLIAM: A pebble.
EVANS: No, it is "lapis"; I pray you remember in your prain.' (*The Merry Wives of Windsor*, Act IV.i.).

speech on the seven ages of man: 'the whining schoolboy, with his satchel/ And shining morning face, creeping like snail/ Unwillingly to school'. The school day was long, from 6 a.m. to 5 p.m., interrupted only briefly for a meal and a quick break. Later, at grammar school, which William would have entered at the age of eleven, pupils had to grapple with the Trivium – grammar, logic and rhetoric. They continued their Latin

The figures on the frontispiece of this Latin primer (1607) symbolize the liberal arts of the Trivium and Quadrivium.

studies, reading classics such
as Ovid's *Metamorphoses*
and *Heroides*, Virgil's
Aeneid, the works of
Cicero, Horace and
Sallust. They also
learned Greek, starting
perhaps with Lucian's
Dialogues, or exercises in
translation of the New
Testament.

Shakespeare's schooling
then came to an end.
Unlike his playwright
contemporaries in London,
the 'university wits', he did
not go to university. This was an age in
which a good grammar school pupil
endowed with a strong intellectual curiosity
could become thoroughly self-educated. The fact
that he lacked higher education and social advantages
indeed proved no obstacle to Shakespeare. His love of
language and innate mastery of the art of the theatre,
combined with a tremendous capacity for work and
fertile powers of invention, were enough to enable
him to produce work of astonishing range.

The rural world, the seasons, the cycle of life

A descendant of farming stock, Shakespeare was
steeped in rural tradition. There is frequent reference
in his works to nature, flowers, trees, animals. Plants
and flowers are used with powerful symbolic effect in
the queen's famous speech on Ophelia's death in
Hamlet (Act IV.vii.), following the scene in which the
girl, stricken by madness, hands out flowers
and herbs. In plays such as *Romeo and
Juliet*, *A Midsummer Night's Dream*,
Othello, *The Winter's Tale*, and
also in the imagery of the
Sonnets, the

The herbals of the
period, such as that
of John Gerard, included
illustrations of herbs and
flowers (left and right).
Plant and animal life
inspired much
contemporary art,
including the hunting
scene and animal
engravings below. Such
images are frequent in
Shakespeare.

‚HOSTESS: I am no thing to thank God on... thou art a knave to call me so.
FALSTAFF: Setting thy womanhood aside, thou art a beast to say otherwise.
HOSTESS: Say, what beast, thou knave, thou?
FALSTAFF: What

rose, herbs, autumn leaves, are used to evoke the cycle of the seasons and mark the inexorable passage of time.

The animal world is also well represented in Shakespeare. Birds abound: the lark, messenger of

beast? Why, an otter.
PRINCE: An otter, Sir John! Why an otter?
FALSTAFF: Why, she's neither fish nor flesh: a man knows not where to have her.‛

Henry IV, Part 1
Act III.iii.

day, and the nightingale who sings at night. *Macbeth* is characterized by a preponderance of images of nocturnal birds and birds of prey, owls, kites, rooks, vultures, falcons, crows. The Shakespearean bestiary includes bats, serpents, hedgehogs, insects; the latter appear figuratively as the fairy creatures in *A Midsummer Night's Dream* or in the Queen Mab speech in *Romeo and Juliet*. The bestiary also draws on the hunt, including references to a variety of game, hares, wild boar and deer, packs of dogs hot on their heels. In *As You Like It* the sight of a deer mortally wounded inspires an outpouring from Jaques, the moralist of the play.

Shakespeare extends the simple country bestiary to include more exotic species, both foreign and imaginary. He mentions the rhinoceros, the tiger, the elephant, the bear (the last would have been familiar to a Londoner, accustomed to bear-baiting at Bankside) as well as the mythical unicorn, phoenix and dragon. There were also heraldic animals, incorporated in the armorial bearings of the nobility: the bear was the emblem of the Warwicks, for

°You spotted snakes with double tongue,/ Thorny hedgehogs, be not seen;/ Newts and blind-worms, do no wrong,/ Come not near our fairy Queen.°
A Midsummer Night's Dream, Act II.ii.

Trembling to see the ghost of Banquo, whose murder he had ordered, appear at a banquet for his subjects, Macbeth challenges the spectre to assume a form he dare confront, such as that of 'the armed rhinoceros' (*Macbeth*, Act III.iv.), illustrated in this contemporary engraving.

example, and the wild boar that of the Yorks.

Traditional bestiaries laid down an animal hierarchy. The lion, eagle and dolphin symbolized divine kingship, whereas the donkey, pig, goat,

rat and monkey were impure animals, emblems of lechery. Under the influence of theologians specialized in demonology, and in the misogynist climate of the Middle Ages, women were identified with serpents. This link was based not only on the seduction of Eve by the serpent in *Genesis* but also on the physiology of the age, which defined both female and snake as cold and moist. The witch was accompanied by attendants, devilish spirits in animal guise, generally that of a cat or a dog, who sucked her blood and in exchange did her favours or gave her powers.

Over 3000 references to some 180 different species of animal have been identified in Shakespeare's plays, an indication of the extent to which he took his imagery from the animal world. Shakespeare also drew on memories of his Stratford childhood and the imaginary world of the time. His fabulous creatures came straight out of bestiaries and legends. Those on this page are illustrations to Edward Topsell's treatise on *The History of the Serpents* (1608) and *History of Four-Footed Beasts* (1607). The unicorn in the 16th-century Oxburgh tapestry (top left) was a traditional image of chastity and Christ's sacrifice. Sea serpents (left) were an ever-present danger to Elizabethan seafarers. The Hydra (below) figures as a symbol of the multitude in *Coriolanus*.

The hierarchy established in the animal world was reflected in people's culinary habits, underlying for example the rules people observed in Lent, when they gave up meat and ate fish in its place, whether trout, eels or oysters. An association was made between man and meat, woman and fish. These practices were designed to follow the movements of the signs of the Zodiac and the planets, which were believed to regulate man's humours (see p. 104) and govern the different parts of the human body. Shakespeare breathed new life into these beliefs by incorporating them in the daily life of the characters he portrayed, as well as in the folklore, attitudes and symbolism of his plays.

The images drawn from nature work as a whole to enrich the dramatic argument and increase the realism of the plays, which is born of the accumulation of concrete detail. The theatre holds up a mirror to the world, reflecting, in miniature, its motley profusion.

Shakespeare thus never abandoned popular culture, the world of oral tradition, legend and ballad. His rustic scenes are often

fama

Life in Shakespeare's day was anchored in tradition. The two period illustrations on this page can be seen as symbolic of the social structure: the queen (left) pays a visit to the country in all her pomp, while a simple peasant woman (below) takes her geese to market.

The engraving (far left) by Guy Marchant, from *Kalendar and Compost of Shepherds* (1493), illustrates the influence of the planets on different parts of the body. The figure of a fool between the skeleton's legs is in the spirit of the 15th-century Morality Plays.

extraordinarily true to life, as in the dialogue of the carriers in *Henry IV, Part 1* (Act II.i.) before Falstaff and his men attack the pilgrims at Gadshill; or in the sheep-shearing feast in *The Winter's Tale* (Act IV.iv.). His recollections of fairs and markets, of dealers examining livestock, arguing over the price of wool, frequently enliven his plays and give them both vitality and realism.

A visit by the queen

The popular celebrations and traditions accompanying holidays and feast days in the countryside were an opportunity for the young William to enjoy the performances of strolling players. Thanks to its position at a crossroads, Stratford was often visited by well-known troupes: that of the Earl of Leicester in 1573 and 1576, of Lord Strange in 1579, of the Earl of Essex in 1584, and the Queen's Men in 1587. A visit by the queen herself, however, was a wholly different matter. In July 1575 Elizabeth I came in state to

Kenilworth Castle, near Stratford, to
attend lavish festivities laid on for
her by the Earl of Leicester.
The partying, as lavish as it was
brilliant, went on for three
weeks in the presence of the
Court. Open-air
entertainments were
organized for the local people,
come from the surrounding
countryside to greet their
sovereign. Each day, each evening,
brought some cleverly
planned amusement, a mythological
play, or a firework display, all in the finest tradition
of a Renaissance festival. The shows presented in the
queen's honour in the neighbourhood of his native
town must have given Shakespeare many
opportunities to steep himself in theatre and
develop an understanding of its magical effects.

Morris dancers
(above) by
the Thames at
Richmond.

Popular theatre, processions and Mysteries

During the Reformation the wall painting of the *Last
Judgement* decorating the Guild Chapel at Stratford
was whitewashed, which meant that Shakespeare

knew of its existence only from hearsay. Religious holidays and feast days were reduced in number and simplified. Local Puritans objected to the old

In 1591 Elizabeth I visited Elvetham, and the Earl of Hertford held a display of water sports in her honour. A pond was dug in the shape of a crescent moon to evoke Diana, the goddess with whom the queen liked to be associated. This engraving (left) shows the queen, surrounded by the Court, watching the spectacle. The engravings of musicians are 16th-century.

holidays rooted in rural custom and the semi-pagan cycle of the seasons: May Day, with its maypole and the traditional Morris dancing, was openly attacked as a licentious revival of paganism and a manifestation of devil worship. In *The Anatomie of Abuses*, published in 1583, the Puritan pamphleteer Philip Stubbes declared these ancient spring celebrations to be devilish rites. The may blossom used to adorn town squares and streets was repeatedly torn down by aggrieved and zealous ministers. Villagers guilty of cutting trees and branches in the royal forests were punished with fines. Even the hobby-horse became an object of persecution, until it was lost to tradition.

The ancient fertility rites lived on in popular memory nonetheless, and it was in popular culture that Shakespeare's theatre had its roots. Old traditions survived in the form of Mummers' Plays, put on at Christmas and Easter, in the course of which the valiant St George, killed in combat with a giant or a Turkish knight, came back to life, thanks to a bottle of magic elixir, in order to triumph over his enemy. The sacrificial aspect of the death and resurrection of the

The Puritans wrote fiery pamphlets denouncing pagan holidays such as May Day with its maypole dance, illustrated here in Charles I's time. The hobby-horse (top left) was a feature of Morris dances. The *Last Judgement* in the Guild Chapel at Stratford (far left) shows devils pushing the damned into Hell. At the Reformation it was pronounced unedifying to the faithful and was whitewashed. (This watercolour was made from what survived in 1807.)

Winter was the season of banquets and indoor entertainments. These early 17th-century watercolours of tavern life show a meal (left) and card-playing (right). At Christmas, actors and fools put on impromptu performances in the houses of the nobility, a piece of improvised theatre or a morning concert, or they might instead mingle with the dancers in disguise. The maskers arriving in this watercolour (right) recall the opening scenes of *Romeo and Juliet* (Act I.ii–iv.), when Romeo, Mercutio and their friends disguise themselves and go to the ball given by old Capulet: 'This night I hold an old accustom'd feast,/ Whereto I have invited many a guest,/ Such as I love…./ At my poor house look to behold this night/ Earth-treading stars that make dark heaven light…. *Enter Romeo, Mercutio, Benvolio, with five or six other Maskers; Torch-bearers.*'

hero, enacted here in the semi-pagan context of popular festivities, is also found in the Mystery Plays of the Middle Ages. Scenes from the Old and New Testaments were acted out on travelling stages, presenting the death and resurrection of Christ for the people of York, Coventry and Chester. These performances were held on the feast of Corpus Christi. Instituted in 1264 by Pope Urban IV, this was the last moveable holy day in the religious calendar, falling between 21 May and 24 June. The time of year meant the plays could be acted in their entirety in daylight.

In addition to grandiloquent declamations by characters such as Herod – Hamlet refers to an actor who 'out-Herods Herod' (Act III.ii.) – the plays featured boisterous squabbles between Noah and his wife, a streak of realism, and bawdy humour accompanying the entrance of the devils. The Morality Plays of the 15th century became more secular in their handling of religious themes, introducing allegorical figures such as Everyman, Charity, Folly, Pleasure. Plays such as *The Castle of Perseverance* were performed by strolling players in stately homes and town halls or on stages erected like the big-top circuses of today.

City processions

The flamboyant spectacles put on in the streets of medieval London and lasting for several days had their origin in the early 'pageants'. After the Reformation, civic processions replaced the earlier, religiously inspired, occasions. They were held on 23 April, St George's Day; 24 June, St John's Day; and 29 October, the day of the Lord Mayor's procession. In a series of often eccentric live tableaux, real and fabulous animals (dromedaries, unicorns, dragons) would pull carts on which actors or groups of children dressed as angels performed. The figures who led the processions were typically disguised as savages, bearing torches or firebrands to clear a passage through the crowd. In London all these spectacles were organized by the guilds, for whom they were an occasion to display wealth and power. It was later that the shows were entrusted to dramatists such as Thomas Dekker, Thomas Heywood and Anthony Munday. The spectacle in this painting (details left) of 1615, by Denis van Asloot, celebrated the Infanta Isabella's entrance into Brussels.

The rich memories of Sir Henry Unton

This anonymous painting, dated 1596, celebrates the life and death of Sir Henry Unton. The scene second from the right (detail below) shows the interior of Unton's house with a masque taking place. A procession advances in a spiral, three groups of ladies ascending the steps in pairs, a bow and a bunch of flowers in the hand, a red mask over the face. In the centre is a small group of musicians. Above them, a winged Mercury stands by Diana, who wears her traditional moon headdress and carries a bow and arrow. Ten cupids – five black and five white, an allegory of night and day – carry torches, which cast a mysterious light over the scene. The rest of the painting depicts Unton's birth, diplomatic career, funeral and monument.

Closely related to the Morality Plays were the Interludes (*Fulgens and Lucrece*, for example), performed between the courses of a banquet. They took the form of long debates on the subject of marriage, punctuated by often obscene or scatological comic scenes acted by clowns known as Vices.

Rites of passage: baptism, marriage and funeral

Little written evidence of Shakespeare's life survives beyond the dates of his baptism and marriage, duly inscribed in the records. What we do know, nonetheless, is that the stages of a person's life were customarily marked at the time by rites of passage valued both as traditions and for their religious significance. These rites, dating back to the Middle Ages, were portrayed in allegorical form in a good number of paintings and engravings, one example of which is the painting (pp. 32–3) of the birth, life and death of Sir Henry Unton. As we have seen, Shakespeare makes reference to the ages of man in *As You Like It*.

The contemporary painting by the Flemish artist Joris Hoefnagel (above right) shows a wedding feast at Bermondsey, a village on the Thames. At Court, nuptial festivities often included a masque, or dramatic entertainment, on an appropriate mythological subject featuring Hymen and Juno; music and dance added to the gaiety of the occasion.

Notwithstanding the Reformation, the religious rites accompanying these various ceremonies had been preserved for an important reason. They were considered necessary to ward off evil spirits and guard against the wicked doings of fairies, who were given to substituting a misshapen child, or changeling, for the fine infant in its cradle.

Full funeral rites were also believed essential to the repose of the soul of the deceased. However, the financial crisis affecting the great English families in the late 16th century led to a reduction in the pomp with which such events were celebrated.

Fairies, witches and other wonders

Goblins, fairies and sprites, such as Puck or Robin Goodfellow, were not particularly well-regarded in the popular belief of the time. They were disturbing little creatures who appeared only at night and played tricks on people, pinching them, driving them mad, luring them into their underground kingdoms, terrifying them with nightmares.

Shakespeare created an important role for these creatures from Celtic folklore, made

From birth to death, cradle to coffin, and finally skeleton, man's life was divided into the seven ages portrayed in this anonymous 16th-century painting (below left). Marriage was a major event and an occasion of exuberant feasting, as seen in the above painting by the 16th-century artist Joris Hoefnagel.

All the world's a stage,/ And all the men and women merely players;/ They have their exits and their entrances;/ And one man in his time plays many parts,/ His acts being seven ages.
As You Like It
Act II.vii.

S hakespeare established himself in London, caught up in the capital's astonishing development. This once small city, numbering some 50,000 in the reign of Henry VIII, underwent a huge influx from the countryside to become a metropolis of 200,000 under Elizabeth I. Overpopulated and filthy, London was a city of spectacle, of theatre, of popular emotion, of seething activity...

CHAPTER 2
LONDON

On Sundays crowds gathered to listen to the sermon at St Paul's cathedral, the subject of this anonymous painting (right) dated 1616. The detail from a 1572 map of London (left) shows closely packed buildings intersected by thoroughfares, with gardens and open spaces on the outskirts.

London in the 16th century

The capital was at that time confined to the City, bordered by the Thames to the south and enclosed by a semicircular wall running from Fleet Ditch in the west to the Tower of London in the east. Within these boundaries lay a labyrinth of little streets crossed by two main thoroughfares, one running east–west from Newgate to Aldgate and passing through the districts of Cheapside, Cornhill and Leadenhall, the other leading from Bishopsgate in the north to London Bridge in the south. The bridge was the only route across the Thames, apart, of course, from the numerous boats that shuttled between its banks. The bulk of the 200,000-strong population was crammed within the City walls. On the top of a hill east of Ludgate stood the old St Paul's cathedral, dominating the town amidst a forest of church towers. St Paul's was the publishing district, where Shakespeare lived for a time. Shopkeepers and craftsmen ran their businesses in the City, which was ruled over by the Lord Mayor. This dignitary was elected

The south bank of the Thames was virtually open ground in 1588, when the watercolour below was painted, showing the infamous district of Bankside and its arenas for animal fights, next to which the Rose and Globe theatres were built. On the north bank, from east to west, one sees the Tower of London inside its own walls, London Bridge,

LONDON.

and the outline of St Paul's; to the west are the palaces of the nobility, as far as Westminster, identifiable by its towers on the far left.

each year by the twelve guilds, each of which was highly jealous of its privileges. The houses and palaces of the nobility, Somerset House, the Savoy, the royal palace and gardens of Whitehall, all lay to the west along the banks of the river as far as Westminster, seat of the Privy Council.

When Shakespeare moved there London was in the throes of expansion. Artisans and shopkeepers were still quite strictly regulated and looked after their employees, who often lived on the premises with them. Work was gruelling, with long hours and few distractions – at any rate within the City walls, as the City Fathers maintained a close watch over public

The church bells rang at the processions held in honour of the Lord Mayor of London (shown in this 17th-century illustration), who was elected annually by the twelve guilds. After the decline of the port of Antwerp in 1585, the port of London flourished. Vessels large and small sailed up and down and across the Thames. The Royal Exchange at Cornhill and St Paul's

cathedral were the centre of busy districts, popular with booksellers and the fashionable world.

morals. Theatres and other places of
entertainment were kept outside the
precincts, relegated to Shoreditch or Bankside,
or to liberties (areas of land outside the City
jurisdiction), such as Blackfriars, which before
the Reformation had belonged to religious
orders. The
City did
nonetheless
have inns
and
taverns
in which
plays were performed: The Bull,
The Bell, The Cross Keys, identified by
their brightly painted signs.

London's southern border, the
Thames, abounded in fish and was
considered the glory and wealth of
the city. More than a river, it was
London's main thoroughfare and
carried much traffic, from royal
barges and large ships to a multiplicity of
smaller boats and skiffs belonging to

Seen from Greenwich, London appears a distant blur behind the Isle of Dogs in the centre (Flemish painting dated 1620). Although the country came up to the city gates, and there were numerous gardens within its walls, nothing could stop the ravages of the plague, the suffering and death. The only treatment, other than bleeding, was rosemary, which people would put in their ears and noses to protect themselves. Houses visited by infection were boarded up and branded with a red cross, their occupants cut off from the outside world whether or not they were ill. In *Romeo and Juliet* (Act V.ii.) Friar John is prevented from delivering a letter to Romeo, telling him of the stratagem of Juliet's pretended death, because guards at Mantua 'Suspecting that we both were in a house/ Where the infectious pestilence did reign, / Sealed up the doors, and would not let us forth'.

the townspeople. The country was not far off: there was Chelsea, Moorfields, Finsbury Fields, a good place for archery practice, and Paddington, a popular destination for a Sunday walk on the green. And westwards along the Strand, as far as the hamlet of Whitehall, parks and gardens were laid out around the palaces.

The plague

Worried to see the population huddling inside the walls as increasing numbers flocked in from the country, the Crown forbade all new building within a radius of three miles of the City. Fields and gardens then became building sites, which compounded the problems of sanitation and paved the way for the plague that was to devastate London.

The pest was seen as the scourge of God on the wickedness of the city. Theatres were immediately closed, the first victim of measures inspired more by the urge for moral order than any effective prevention of disease. The plague ravaged London in 1564, in 1592–3, in 1603 and in 1623, leaving a total of some 100,000 victims in its wake. Death spread from the suburbs to the centre. The bell rang as the cart went by, carrying corpses to their pauper's grave.

The Tower of London and London Bridge

Outside the City walls the theatres and brothels and bear gardens stood side by side. Here, in an atmosphere of carefree anarchy, lived a disreputable crowd of beggars, pickpockets and pedlars. The area was reputed to be dangerous at particular times of

day, though in fact crime seems to have been no greater than it was inside London. To come here one had to pass below the ominous walls of the Tower of London, which held political prisoners, and also the royal menagerie with its famous lions, and an Indian transported from America. One then had to cross the bridge of twenty arches, along the narrow passage for pedestrians and vehicles that ran between the houses.

Shakespeare–Shake-scene

The trail of Shakespeare's life, lost after the record of the baptism of his twins in 1585, reappears indirectly

Men accused of treason were imprisoned in the Tower of London. The impressive fortress with a grim history is shown in this 17th-century engraving (left) by Wenceslaus Hollar. It is to the Tower that the Duke of Clarence in *Richard III* is sent by his brother Edward IV; it is in the Tower that another brother, the Duke of Gloucester, has him murdered. Gloucester also orders the murder of Edward's sons to clear the path to the throne and advises the crown prince 'some day or two/ Your highness shall repose you at the Tower', drawing the reply 'I do not like the Tower, of any place:/ Did Julius Caesar build that place, my lord?' (Act III.i.). In the Renaissance the Tower also housed the royal menagerie of lions and bears. London Bridge, the only route over the Thames, carried rows of houses and shops down each side. The heads of traitors were exhibited on stakes over Bridge Gate as a reminder of the weight of royal justice.

'The Bear garden'   'The Globe'

in 1592 in the shape of a pamphlet by the novelist, poet and playwright Robert Greene (1558–92). Greene gives unique evidence of the young Shakespeare's successful career and much information on the theatrical world of the time, including the rivalries that existed between actors and playwrights and, most of all, between the various companies of players.

In *Groatsworth of Wit Bought with a Million of Repentance*, published three months

The view of London Bridge (above) is dated *c.* 1615, the engraving (below), 1616. In 1599 the Swiss traveller Thomas Platter reported that he had crossed the river with friends, and in a building with a thatched roof (the Globe) had seen *Julius Caesar*.

King Henry the Sixt

This band sets like to the mornings Warre,
When dying clouds contend, with growing light
What time the Shepheard blowing of his nailes,
Can neither call it perfect day, nor night.
Now swayes it this way, like a Mighty Sea,
Forc'd by the Tide, to combat with the Winde:
Now swayes it that way, like the selfe-same Sea,
Forc'd to retyre by fury of the Winde.
Sometime, the Flood prevayles, and then the Winde:
Now, one the better, then another best,
Both tugging to be Victors, brest to brest,
Yet neither Conqueror, nor Conquered.
So is the equall poise of this fell Warre.

after his death, Greene attacks Shakespeare as 'an upstart crow, beautified with our feathers' and goes on to refer in even more extreme terms to 'his Tygers heart wrapt in a Players hide' (see p. 146). This is a parody of the line in Shakespeare's *Henry VI, Part 3* (Act I.iv.) where the Duke of York addresses Queen Margaret: 'O tiger's heart wrapp'd in a woman's hide!'

Greene further asserts that 'he [Shakespeare] is as well able to bumbast out a blanke verse as the best of you; and being an absolute *Johannes Factotum*, is in his owne conceit the onely Shake-scene in a countrie' – an obvious insult, as well as a rather poor pun on Shakespeare's name.

In Shakespeare's day the writer was commonly a drudge, obliged to hire out his services to anyone in a position to pay him money or house him in return. There were no newspapers, and the writer's craft was unprofitable. The learned Doctor Faustus (below), tired of study, and yearning to discover the secrets of the universe, sold his soul to the devil in exchange for the worldly power and pleasure that only gold could obtain. Outside the Court, the only path to success was to produce plays capable of drawing audiences of two thousand at each performance.

The Tragicall Histor
of the Life and Death
of Doctor FAVSTVS.

With new Additions.

Written by *Ch. Mar.*

His contemporaries, friends and masters

Shakespeare did not simply appear from nowhere in a literary desert. By the 16th century the theatre had become an institution, and a group of educated young people set out to make it their career. The first of these was John Lyly

(1544–1606), author also of mannered novels whose main character, Euphues, gave his name to the florid rhetorical style known as 'euphuism'. Lyly's plays are mythological entertainments, for example *Endymion* (1591) and *Galathea* (1592), or comedies full of folklore, such as *Mother Bombie* (1594). Performed by companies of boys, they were highly successful at Court.

George Peele (1556–96) is best known for two works, *The Arraignment of Paris* (1584), a pastoral comedy in the form of a masque, and *The Old Wives' Tale* (1595), which employs the device of a play within a play and is also interesting for its use of chivalric

elements. The plays of Shakespeare's unhappy rival Robert Greene combined historical tales with fantasy, interweaving several strands of plot and sub-plot.

But the development of Elizabethan drama was due above all to Christopher Marlowe (1564–93) and Thomas Kyd, both of whom wrote tragedies of high drama and emotion. Marlowe's lines, delivered by an actor of the calibre of Edward Alleyn, for example, would resound through the pit of the Rose Theatre. Marlowe's death at the age of twenty-eight, stabbed in the eye during a tavern brawl, put a brutal end to a highly promising career. His heroes, the conquering Tamburlaine, the visionary Faustus, driven by the desire to push back the frontiers of knowledge and the human condition, made Marlowe the very incarnation of Renaissance man.

Kyd's play *The Spanish Tragedy* was a revenge tragedy, the first in a genre that many were to take up after him. Its hero, the old Hieronimo, pretends madness and uses a theatrical performance as a stratagem to achieve a vengeance as spectacular as it is bloody. Shakespeare was to remember this work when he wrote *Titus Andronicus*.

All these playwrights knew success before Shakespeare arrived on the scene. But the premature death of Marlowe left the field open and gave the man from Stratford every opportunity, as Greene declared in his pamphlet, to beautify himself with the feathers of his illustrious predecessors.

Shakespeare's astonishing rise

A member of the best theatrical company of the time, and early free of rivals, Shakespeare could look

The portrait opposite, dated 1585, is said to be of Christopher Marlowe. Above is the so-called 'Chandos' portrait of Shakespeare. When Shakespeare arrived in London, it was the powerful lines of Marlowe that filled the Rose Theatre. The son of a Canterbury cobbler, he was a precocious genius who had written major works by the age of twenty-seven. His early death may have been politically motivated, as he was employed by the Crown as a spy. Shakespeare stepped into his shoes as a dramatist. The three parts of *Henry VI* show him to have been strongly influenced by Marlowe's superb oratorical style.

Executions were held in public on a raised platform, as seen in this engraving taken from the first edition (1577) of Raphael Holinshed's *Chronicles*. The condemned were entitled to make a speech to the crowd before they died: a bloody form of theatre which Shakespeare made use of in *Henry VI* and *Richard III*.

The Merchan

forward to an immediate and undiluted success. His rise marked the triumph of a new generation of professionals in the theatre.

Between 1590 and 1597 he principally wrote historical dramas. These fall into two tetralogies, the first of which comprises *Henry VI, Parts 1–3,* and *Richard III*, and the second *Richard II, Henry IV, Parts 1–2,* and *Henry V*. He also wrote the single play *King John*, set in the early 12th century. Shakespeare found his inspiration in the work of the contemporary historian Raphael Holinshed, author of *Chronicles of England, Scotland and Ireland*. These were published

in 1577 and reissued in 1587 with plates and *marginalia* intended to make them more attractive and easier of reference.

Overlapping with these history plays, between 1593 and 1600, Shakespeare put onto the stage ten comedies, which range from farce to romance: *The Comedy of Errors, The Taming of the Shrew* and

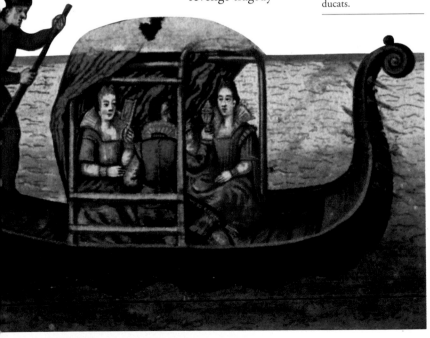

The Merry Wives of Windsor keep company with the more lyrical *A Midsummer Night's Dream* and *The Merchant of Venice*, to end on the somewhat disenchanted note of *Twelfth Night*.

In the tragic mode he meanwhile produced only *Titus Andronicus*, a bloody revenge tragedy

Many of Shakespeare's comedies originate in popular tales or farces in which the world is turned inside out; an example is *The Taming of the Shrew*, in which Petruchio has to find a way of taming his wife Catherine's temper. The comedies of the mature years, notably *The Merchant of Venice*, deal with more serious subjects, such as the nature of justice. There we see the Jew Shylock ready to take his pound of flesh from the body of the merchant Antonio, who is unable to repay his debt of a thousand ducats.

of Venice.

inspired by Seneca and Thomas Kyd, and *Romeo and Juliet*, a drama of passion and comedy which ends unhappily. With rare exceptions, Shakespeare never invented the plots or characters of his plays. Apart from folklore, he found his subjects in the writings of others, while ever ready to make major changes to suit the story to the stage and increase its dramatic impact. This approach also enabled him to tackle the burning issues and topical themes of his day, from national history to romantic intrigue, to vengeance, to madness, to witchcraft. The resounding success of most of his works confirmed that his talent had served him well.

Shakespeare, actor, writer and shareholder

Robert Greene's attack on Shakespeare had its roots in the rivalries plaguing Lord Strange's Men, the troupe to which Shakespeare belonged, who were then playing in the Rose Theatre owned by Philip Henslowe. In the detailed record of performances and takings kept by the latter, he mentions two plays by Greene: a comedy, *The Honourable History of Friar Bacon and Friar Bungay*, performed on 19 February

1592, and a tragedy, *Orlando Furioso*, performed shortly after. Neither work seems to have been popular. In contrast, on Friday 3 March he mentions a play that, to judge by the takings, was an outright success: 'harey the vi', probably *Henry VI, Part 2*.

Unfortunately, on the heels of these glorious beginnings, a violent epidemic of the plague broke out. Public theatres were again closed by the city authorities; the existing troupes were disbanded, the actors scattered. Forced to give up the theatre, Shakespeare wrote two narrative poems, *Venus and Adonis* and *The Rape of Lucrece*, dedicating them to his patron Henry Wriothesley, Earl of Southampton.

The portrait above left is of Ferdinando, Lord Strange, the fifth Earl of Derby, whose company of players performed *Henry VI* at the Rose Theatre, according to Henslowe's accounts (extract above).

The battle scene (top) is dated *c.* 1615 and the engraving of the Gorgons (left), 1610.

The story of the two cruelly fated lovers Pyramus and Thisbe, portrayed in this engraving dated 1538, is told by Ovid in *Metamorphoses*. It inspired Chaucer and later Shakespeare, who wrote his first, tragic, version of the same basic story in *Romeo and Juliet*, followed by the burlesque rendering in the play presented to Theseus' court by a group of craftsmen at the end of *A Midsummer Night's Dream*. A playwright had to master every register, to move from laughter to tears, as Shakespeare did, by simple changes of perspective and atmosphere.

He returned to the stage at the end of 1594 as one of the company of the Chamberlain's Men. With him were the actors William Kemp and Richard Burbage. They put on two performances of *The Comedy of Errors* for the Court during the Christmas festivities. Lord Strange had died on 16 April 1593, and in 1594 his company passed into the hands of the Lord Chamberlain, Henry Carey, basing itself at the Theatre, James Burbage's playhouse in Bishopsgate, north of the city walls. It severed its connection with Philip Henslowe and the popular actor Edward Alleyn, the star of Marlowe's tragedies. These two men now moved their allegiance to the Lord Admiral, Lord Howard of Effingham, and established themselves at the Rose Theatre.

The Chamberlain's Men were organized in an unusual manner: the six main actors formed an association in which each was a shareholder, directly receiving part of the takings from performances. The actors were financially independent, paying only rent to the theatre proprietor James Burbage. This was in contrast to the Admiral's Men, where the actors were paid by Henslowe, who advanced them money in order to keep a tighter rein on them.

LVCRECE.

LONDON.
Printed by Richard Field, for Iohn Harrison, and are to be sold at the signe of the white Greyhound in Paules Churh yard. 1594.

S hakespeare's interest in tragedy was already apparent in the dark themes of his poem *The Rape of Lucrece* (above).

THE MOST LA mentable Romaine Tragedie of Titus Andronicus:

As it was Plaide by the Right Ho- nourable the Earle of *Darbie*, Earle of *Pembrooke*, and Earle of *Suffex* their Seruants.

LONDON,

Shakespeare never changed company, a fact rare enough to be worthy of note. From now on he worked to strengthen his position as both player and playwright. In addition to his acting he wrote an average of two plays a year until 1608, when the pace of theatrical production slackened. The decision early in his career to remain in one place, with one company, enabled him quickly to consolidate his first successes as a writer and to become in his lifetime the most highly sought-after dramatist of the Elizabethan and Jacobean stage.

T he drawing below left, dated 1595, is the only contemporary illustration of a scene from Shakespeare's plays. It appears on a page bearing some forty lines of *Titus Andronicus* and signed in the left margin by Henry Peacham, tutor and artist. In the centre the queen of the Goths, Tamora, begs Titus to spare the life of her two sons. On the right the Moor Aaron stands with a sword in his left hand. The costumes worn by Titus and Tamora are vaguely historical, while those of the guards are Elizabethan.

The theatre, a path to success

The man whom Greene had termed an upstart soon showed a taste for wealth, particularly land and property. He had a keen eye to profit and mercilessly pursued any defaulting debtors. Shakespeare's name appears both on tax registers and in a variety of legal disputes with his neighbours. This is how we know that from 1599 he lived for a time on the other side of the Thames, in Southwark, near the new Globe Theatre; his name appears on the Bishop of Winchester's registers as a bad taxpayer.

In 1602 he bought 50 hectares of land, and in 1605 a share in the Stratford tithe farm for the fairly considerable sum of £440, which was to bring him some £60 per year. His poetry had earned him the generosity of his patron the

Earl of Southampton, who is said to have given him £1000 for *Venus and Adonis* and *The Rape of Lucrece*. This was an enormous sum for the time, and the theatre must have brought him even greater rewards. Penniless when he left his native town, Shakespeare found himself some twenty-five years later enjoying one of the largest fortunes in Stratford.

The gentleman player

In 1596 Shakespeare applied for the right to bear a coat of arms, renewing the application that had been made by his father, without success, over twenty-five years earlier. This desire for social recognition was not unusual: a number of actors in William Shakespeare's company, Burbage, Heminge, Cowley and Pope, had been granted coats of arms, as had Richard Quiney, another native of Stratford, whose son Thomas was to marry Shakespeare's daughter Judith in 1616.

This time the Shakespeare family obtained its armorial bearings. The rough draft preserved at the College of Arms shows that the petition was granted in recognition of 'the good and loyal service' rendered to the Crown by the family's forebears. Through his great success in the theatre, Shakespeare, the grandson of a farmer, was now a London gentleman.

Henry Wriothesley, Earl of Southampton (left), was the patron to whom Shakespeare dedicated the poems written in the months when the theatres were shut down because of the plague. The coat of arms granted to Shakespeare, shown above and in the document below, dated 1596, was 'in a field of gold upon a bend sable, a spear of the first, the point upward, headed argent', the crest 'a falcon, with his wings displayed, standing on a wreath of his colours', with the motto 'Non sanz droict'.

Gentleman, playwright, actor, one of the Chamberlain's Men, Shakespeare knew how to exploit to the full the resources of contemporary theatre. The variety of settings, the wealth of *dramatis personae*, the heterogeneous nature of the audiences, were all in place for the production of his greatest works.

CHAPTER 3

THE WORLD OF THEATRE

This 18th-century watercolour of the Globe (left) was done from an engraving of 1616. Carved on the front of the theatre was a quotation from Petronius: '*totus mundus agit histrionem*', or, in Shakespeare's words, 'All the world's a stage'. The character of the fool is another aspect of the same idea. In this portrait (right) of Tom Skelton, dated *c.* 1659, he wears the traditional motley dress.

London, where the permanent playhouses were built – the Theatre, the Curtain Theatre, and later the Rose, the Swan, the Globe, the Fortune – had overtaken the provinces, where the Mysteries, Morality Plays and Interludes had developed. This marked a break with the past, although not many good plays were performed from 1576 to 1584. Between 1584 and 1593 the masterpieces were Marlowe's *Tamburlaine* and Kyd's *The Spanish Tragedy.*

The Theatre and the Curtain Theatre, north of the city walls, were the oldest. They belonged to James Burbage, a carpenter by trade. On the other side of the Thames, west of Southwark, Philip Henslowe built the Rose Theatre in 1587. Following in Henslowe's footsteps, Francis Langley, a goldsmith by trade, built the Swan in 1595. This theatre was without a resident company, however, and had difficulty competing with the Admiral's Men and the Chamberlain's Men. It was closed down after the performance in July 1597, by

The Red Bull
(Playhouse)

CLERKENWELL
Priory of
St John
(3rd Revels
Office)

HOLBORN

to The Cockpit
(Phoenix)
(in Drury Lane)

to Westminster

Temple Bar

Whitefriars

Fleet
Ditch

Ludgate

Salisbury
Court

Bell
Savage
Inn

Blackfriars
(2nd Revels
Office & Theatre)

le Playe houfe

R i

The Swa

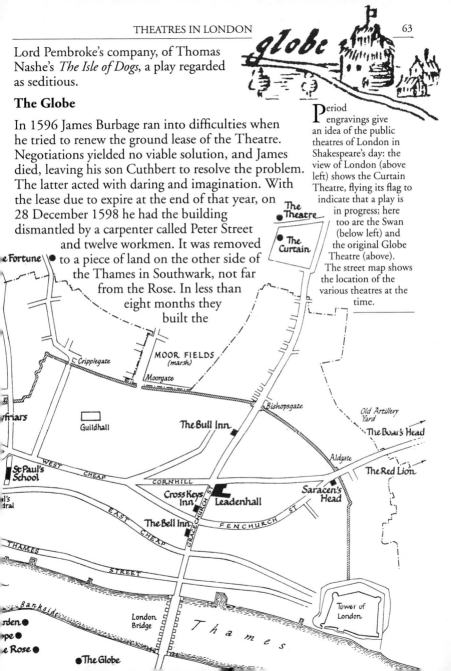

Lord Pembroke's company, of Thomas Nashe's *The Isle of Dogs*, a play regarded as seditious.

The Globe

In 1596 James Burbage ran into difficulties when he tried to renew the ground lease of the Theatre. Negotiations yielded no viable solution, and James died, leaving his son Cuthbert to resolve the problem. The latter acted with daring and imagination. With the lease due to expire at the end of that year, on 28 December 1598 he had the building dismantled by a carpenter called Peter Street and twelve workmen. It was removed to a piece of land on the other side of the Thames in Southwark, not far from the Rose. In less than eight months they built the

Period engravings give an idea of the public theatres of London in Shakespeare's day: the view of London (above left) shows the Curtain Theatre, flying its flag to indicate that a play is in progress; here too are the Swan (below left) and the original Globe Theatre (above). The street map shows the location of the various theatres at the time.

Globe, the splendid 'wooden O'
mentioned by the chorus at the
beginning of *Henry V*. A new type
of association was formed between
the owner of the land, Sir
Nicholas Brend, the two Burbage
brothers Cuthbert and Richard, and the
five players in the Chamberlain's company.
One of these was Shakespeare, who thus became a
'householder', in other words owner of a share in
the property.

The following year, suffering from the competition
provided by the new theatre, Philip Henslowe too
made a move across the Thames – in the opposite
direction. He built the Fortune Theatre to the north
of Cripplegate, in the liberty of Finsbury, on a piece
of land that his son-in-law Edward Alleyn had bought
in 1599. Then in 1613 Henslowe embarked on

This 17th-century
engraving is of bull-
baiting, a popular sport.
In *Troilus and Cressida*
(Act V.vii.) the satirical
Thersites, watching the
fight between Paris and
Menelaus, cries 'The
cuckold and the
cuckold-maker are at it.
Now, bull! now, dog!
'Loo, Paris, 'loo!'

Bear-baiting (below) is another frequent source for Shakespeare's imagery. The bear was tethered to a stake in the ring, into which dogs were released for the attack. A bear might kill a number of the dogs before himself, occasionally, falling prey to their jaws. A 16th-century engraving (left) shows two of the arenas used for the sport. In *Julius Caesar* (Act IV.i.) Octavius cries to Anthony: 'we are at the stake,/ And bay'd about with many enemies'. And in *Macbeth* (Act V.vii.), when Macbeth is cornered by Malcolm's army, his words invoke the same image: 'They have tied me to a stake; I cannot fly,/ But bear-like I must fight the course.'

another major building project, turning the Bear Garden in west Bankside into the Hope, a theatre that could be used both for animal fights and theatrical performances.

The architecture of public theatres

All theatres were destroyed in 1642 and 1644 under order of Parliament. Architectural historians attempting to reconstruct them have had to extract what information they can from drawings, sketches, contracts and any other documents to have survived. The playhouses were 12 metres in height and round or octagonal in shape, with a diameter of some 25 metres. Allowing a depth of 4 metres for the three-tiered galleries and boxes, the auditorium itself could not have occupied much more than 20 metres, into which space there projected, by 8 metres, a raised rectangular stage 12 metres wide. The cramped dimensions are striking. No more than twelve actors could appear on stage at a time because of the space restrictions.

Watercolour of the Globe (opposite, above) by George Shepherd.

Het Haene gefecht

ngeland

The Cockpit

'Can this cockpit hold the vasty fields of France?' asks the chorus in *Henry V*. The cockpits, close to the playhouses on Bankside, were in effect round theatres, where the spectators sat in a circle watching the feathered combat in the centre and placing their bets. They were no less fascinated and involved than audiences at the Globe. This cockfighting scene was painted in 1615. According to Thomas Platter of Basel, the bets could amount to a considerable sum, and the fight last for four or five hours. The Cockpit was also the name of a private theatre in Drury Lane.

The Fortune, the Globe and the Theatre were able to accommodate audiences of between two and three thousand.

Internal layout

Every theatre had the same basic structure, consisting of a stage partially covered by a thatched roof supported by two pillars. In Shakespeare's theatre the roof was embellished with a globe and the Latin inscription '*totus mundus agit histrionem*' ('All the world's a stage'). The stage projected into an uncovered central area within a covered

It is to a Dutchman, Arend van Buchell, that we owe this drawing (below) of the Swan Theatre, realized from a sketch that his friend Johannes de Witt made in 1596. Van Buchell observed that 'the largest and most remarkable of the theatres in London is the Swan, which is able to accommodate three thousand spectators'.

enclosure, which was made up of three tiers of galleries with actors' dressing rooms at the back. The gallery above the stage was independent of the rest and could be used either by the audience or the musicians, or as an additional part of the stage (for the balcony scene in *Romeo and Juliet*, for example). The frontage of the *mimorum aedes*, the actors' tiring house, was broken by two doors for entrances and exits. In the front of the stage there was a trap door used for devilish apparitions and disappearances, and also for burials. A balcony crowned by a gable on the floor above housed the stage machinery. It was from here that gods and goddesses and other supporting characters and effects descended onto the stage. When a play was in progress, the theatre flew a flag above the roof bearing its emblem.

The Elizabethan stage

In Shakespeare's day the stage relied on convention rather than illusion, using a limited number of portable props, scrupulously inventoried by Henslowe in his diary: not only tables, chairs, swords,

The Globe was subject to greater constraints than the more sophisticated Rose Theatre (reconstructed above), judging by the Prologue of *Henry V*: '... may we cram/ Within this wooden O the very casques/ That did affright the air at Agincourt?' Below: drawing, possibly of a stage set, by Philip Henslowe.

Cupid's bows, canvases of the sun and moon, a rock and a monument, but also a head of Mohammed, a rainbow, Mercury's wand, a tree of golden apples, a series of dragons and a cauldron for the Jew (a reference to the end of Marlowe's *The Jew of Malta*, in which Barabas is thrown into a cauldron of boiling oil). Changes of scene were indicated in the text or by a simple placard. For night scenes, inevitably problematic in an open-air playhouse, a simple candle or torch symbolically transported the audience into the nocturnal world. As the chorus says at the beginning of *Henry V*, the theatre relies more on the 'imaginary forces' of the audience than on

The physician Robert Fludd (1574–1637) produced strange engravings of imaginary stage sets such as the one below, perhaps inspired by the Globe. The images are mnemonic: the five doors onto the stage are intended to recall to the mind texts that the scholar wishes to remember. The five circles and lozenges on the floor are more mysterious.

realistic effects. The text sufficed to bring the play to life. Thus, in *King Lear* (Act IV.vi.), for example, Edgar convinces his blind father Gloucester that he is on the edge of a cliff, from which the latter intends to jump, by describing what is supposedly visible below – crows no bigger than insects, men the size of mice: 'How fearful/ And dizzy 'tis to cast one's eyes so low!/ The crows and choughs that wing the midway air/ Show scarce so gross as

•When we are born, we cry that we are come/ To this great stage of fools.•
King Lear, Act IV.iii.

beetles..../ The fishermen that walk upon the beach/ Appear like mice....' In the empty space, the symbolic void of the stage, the only note of warmth was provided by the magnificence of the costumes.

An orchestra accompanied the unfolding of a play with a varied range of sound effects and instruments; drums and trumpets, for example, served to heighten the excitement of battle scenes.

At the end of the performance the actors would often improvise a sung satirical farce, danced in time to a jig.

The audience

Thanks to the wide range of prices offered by the 'box offices' of the time, theatres were places of popular entertainment. Entrance to the pit – standing room round the stage – cost only a

A theatre stage as illustrated in 1632 on the title page of William Alabaster's play *Roxana*.

THE TRAGEDIE OF
IVLIVS CÆSAR.

Cæf. Et Tu Brute———— *Then fall Cæfar.*

penny; prices rose to sixpence for seated places in the covered galleries. The first were within reach of all pockets, representing scarcely one-twelfth of a London worker's weekly salary. The second were the preserve of rich city merchants and the nobility. (Sixpence also happened to be the price of a quarto edition of a play.)

Audiences were highly diverse. The Puritans railed at the rogues, pickpockets and prostitutes to be found in their midst, and regarded the theatres as places of ill-repute, no better than the neighbouring brothels. The motley and bustling crowd of spectators ate and

• Suit the action to the word, the word to the action; with this special observance, that you o'erstep not the modesty of nature; for anything so o'erdone is from the purpose of playing, whose end, both at the first and now, was and is to hold, as 'twere, the mirror up to nature.
Hamlet, Act III.ii.

•FALSTAFF: I was as virtuously given as a gentleman need to be; virtuous enough: swore little, dic'd not above seven times a week, went to a bawdy house not above once in a quarter… of an hour.•
Henry IV, Part 1
Act III.iii.

drank during the performance and gave free rein to their emotions, roaring with laughter, dissolving into tears. They had a relish for language and were much stirred by the long speeches delivered in verse by such actors as Alleyn or Burbage, the stars of the Rose and the Globe.

The actors

Professional actors were a novelty in late 16th-century England, and often much admired. Until then players had been amateurs, members of guilds who acted in Morality Plays and Mysteries on the feast of Corpus Christi, supplemented by the travelling jugglers and mime artists who performed at fairs and on village greens. In *A Midsummer Night's Dream*, for example, when Bottom and his company rehearse the drama of 'Pyramus and Thisbe', hoping to be permitted to play it at Court on the occasion of the marriage of Duke Theseus, the actors are all craftsmen in various fields: weaver, carpenter, tailor and bellows-mender.

The situation changed when the government began to take measures to control vagrancy and delinquency. An order was passed in 1572 that made an actor into a potential suspect, liable to be thrown into prison and branded with a hot iron if he were caught. This made it essential for a player to join the company of a prominent figure and bear his livery and arms.

The Chamberlain's Men comprised eight main shareholders, rising to twelve in 1604, after Elizabeth's death. The company was then taken under the wing of the new sovereign and became known as the King's Men. They had the honour of marching in the celebrations organized for James I's entry into London.

The size of each actor's shareholding was proportionate to the sum he had invested in the business for the purchase of the basic stock, props and costumes, of which he was joint owner. The shareholders divided between them half of the takings from the gallery seats, while the other half went towards the costs and upkeep of the theatre. Though the total obviously varied, it often proved substantial. In addition to the hard core of the company, hired men would play minor roles for a weekly salary that was less than the average earnings of a craftsman. Others were engaged as watchmen, wardrobe-keepers, property-men, copyists, musicians and prompters.

Players in the King's Men: from left to right, John Lowin, William Sly, and Nathan Field, who probably replaced Shakespeare when he died.

⁕Wee … doe licence and aucthorize theise our Servauntes Lawrence Fletcher, William Shakespeare, Richard Burbage, Augustyne Phillippes, Iohn Heninges, Henrie Condell, William Sly, Robert Armyn, Richard Cowly, and the rest of theire Associates freely to use and exercise the Arte and faculty of playing Comedies, Tragedies, histories, Enterludes, moralls, pastoralls, Stageplaies….⁕

James I
Letter patent of 1603

Actor John Green (left, c. 1608) won fame on his tours in Germany and Austria in 1607–8.

At the time of Shakespeare's death the King's Men consisted of twenty-six permanent actors – a considerable number for the time.

Female roles

The theatrical companies included five or six boys or adolescents trained to play female roles until such time as their voices broke. They learnt their trade from the most practised actors and were well paid as long as the theatres flourished. But their prospects were uncertain: at puberty, when they could no longer wear wigs and dresses, they often had no future other than as humble company employees.

These youths were nonetheless true professionals, who from a very young age learnt singing, dancing, music, diction, and feminine gestures and intonation. Contemporary audiences found them wholly convincing. Their parts were difficult, however, as well as specialized. It is therefore no surprise that, given the preponderance of adults in the companies, Shakespeare's plays have fewer female than male characters.

The clowns

The clown was another specialized role. On the Elizabethan stage a distinction was made between the clown and the fool. The former was a rough peasant whose blunders served as a counterbalance to the heroic or romantic language of the other characters. The latter was a professional jester fitted out in motley, cap and bells.

In a comical scene from *A Midsummer Night's Dream* (Act I.ii.), the craftsmen of Athens, eager to perform 'Pyramus and Thisbe' at Court, seem nonetheless reluctant to play female parts: 'QUINCE: Flute, you must take Thisby on you.

FLUTE: What is Thisby? A wand'ring knight?
QUINCE: It is the lady that Pyramus must love.
FLUTE: Nay, faith, let not me play a woman; I have a beard coming.'

Hoftes

In 1588 the clown Richard Tarlton died. The sparkling repartee and humour of this deformed and flat-nosed dwarf had made him famous throughout London and amused even the queen. He was replaced, a little later, by the clown William Kemp, who joined the Chamberlain's Men. He performed marvellously as Launcelot Gobbo in *The Merchant of Venice* and as Dogberry, the stupid constable in *Much Ado About Nothing*. After Kemp left the company in 1600 Shakespeare engaged Robert Armin, a slight, intelligent little man, for whom he wrote jesting parts, such as that of Touchstone in *As You Like It*, and roles that

Richard Tarlton, the queen's favourite clown, is portrayed in peasant dress, playing a pipe and drum in the above drawing of *c.* 1588 by John Scottowe. The other illustrations are from the title page of *The Wits* (1673) by Francis Kirkman, a collection of comic scenes from popular plays.

displayed an acrobatic wit, one of which was the fool in *King Lear*. Behind his capers and verbal games, the fool gives the king a bitter lesson in wisdom.

The actor's art

All these actors required a combination of talent and dedication to their craft, for the theatres were commercial enterprises dependent on the success of the plays they performed. And competition was fierce. In season – in other words outside Lent, when the theatres were closed – actors performed every afternoon except on Sunday. They also had regularly to vary their repertoire, and generally had no more than two weeks in which to prepare a new play. And they often found themselves playing several roles, particularly when on tour, with the troupe reduced to a minimum. This demanded quick work and an excellent memory.

The clown William Kemp danced for nine days on the road from London to Norwich, as illustrated in the above title page of his *Nine Daies Wonder* (1600). Plays often ended with a jig, and with the audience going off to slake their thirst in a nearby tavern (below). An early 17th-century painting (right) shows a common image of a clown with a pair of bellows or, in Latin, *follis*, a form of visual pun.

Etiam astro dormienti

Dic mihi, qualis eris?

Fashionable emblems

The panels painted by Lady Drury at Hawstead, her house near Bury St Edmunds in Suffolk, were clearly inspired by engravings in contemporary books of emblems, such as those by Geoffrey Whitney (1586) and Claude Paradin (1591). These compilations all followed the same pattern: one emblem per page, with a Latin motto above, an engraving in the centre, of moral, allegorical or enigmatic import, and a brief commentary on the image below. Lady Drury's panels feature only a restrained scroll bearing a Latin saying. The sleeping figure in the left-hand panel surely represents sloth, though it can also be seen as an illustration of Bottom, transformed into a donkey in *A Midsummer Night's Dream*. The right-hand painting calls to mind the central metaphor of Shakespeare's sonnet no. 24: 'Mine eye hath play'd the painter and hath stell'd/ Thy beauty's form in table of my heart;/ My body is the frame wherein 'tis held,/ And perspective it is best painter's art.'

Reason in madness

One of Whitney's emblems was entitled *Aethiopem lavare* (to wash the Ethiopian), the moral of which was that one cannot change the colour bestowed on one by nature, however hard one tries. This was clearly the inspiration of the panel far left by Lady Drury. In *Titus Andronicus* (Act IV.ii.), Aaron, the evil-minded Moor, defends the colour of his skin, or more precisely that of the illegitimate child that Tamora, queen of the Goths, has just had by him: 'Coal-black is better than another hue/ In that it scorns to bear another hue;/ For all the water in the ocean/ Can never turn the swan's black legs to white,/ Although she lave them hourly in the flood.' The ship about to be capsized by a whale (above), beneath the motto *Nusquam tuta fides* (you cannot rely on promises), recalls the opening scene in *The Tempest*, where Antonio and the courtiers of Milan discover to their stupefaction that the enraged waves seem only to mock the authority of the king. The old man (left) beside the motto *Desipui sapiendo* (through my wisdom, I am foolish), suggests King Lear on the barren heath.

In 1594–5 the Admiral's Men performed thirty-eight plays, twenty-one of which were new.

The public and the actors

Those who frequented the theatre, and in particular the pit – which meant standing throughout 'the two hours' traffic' of a performance, as the prologue to *Romeo and Juliet* calls it – were eager for sensation and overwhelming emotion. They loved impassioned grandiloquence, metaphor and extremes. It was impossible to mumble words to jostling and undisciplined spectators: their attention had to be captured.

A taste for thrills and horror was deeply embedded in popular audiences. Hence the success of revenge tragedies, rich in macabre scenes and spectacular effects. The strength of national feeling, stirred by the defeat of the Spanish Armada in 1588, and the craze for English history, revealed by the success of a play such as Marlowe's *Edward II*, is further evidenced by the popularity of the highly coloured scenes represented in chronicles and history plays. The din of battle, the clash of weapons, evoked strong

There were many books about duelling and its rules in the Renaissance, among them George Silver's *Paradoxes of Defence* (1599). The illustration of a duel below is from 1616. In the theatre duels and combats, for instance that between Mercutio and Tybalt in *Romeo and Juliet*, or between Edgar and his half-brother Edmund at the end of *King Lear*, were carefully arranged and highly popular with audiences of the period. In comedies such as *As You Like It* and *Twelfth Night* the duel was presented as a dangerous passion and the absurd fashion of another age.

emotion, while heroic deeds were an occasion to show actors in hand-to-hand combat.

Gone were the days of the brave strolling players, generally limited to four adults and two boys, with each actor playing several parts. The two largest public theatres in London and the private theatres – in other words theatres with a covered auditorium – staged very different plays, each with its particular style, and its own 'regulars'. Edward Alleyn, attached to the Rose and then the Fortune, was famous for his declamatory manner. Shakespeare, on the other hand, wrote complex parts for Richard Burbage, such as that of the prince in *Hamlet*, who reveals various different aspects of his character as the play unfolds. As an actor, Shakespeare was content to play the more minor roles, for example that of Adam, the old servant in *As You Like It*, or the ghost of the king in *Hamlet*.

Richard Burbage (1568–1619), also a talented artist, probably painted this self-portrait (left). He was the son of James Burbage, who built the Theatre, and a star performer in the Chamberlain's Men. He played all the great parts in Shakespeare's tragedies – Hamlet, Othello, King Lear. An anecdote recorded in 1602 by the lawyer John Manningham related that when he was playing Richard III a lady in the audience invited him to her house. Overhearing this, Shakespeare hurried to get there before him. And when Burbage presented himself at the lady's door, it was to be informed that

HAMLET, Prince of Denmarke.

Alas poore *Torick*, I knew him *Horatio*

The Tragedie of King Lear.

poore *Tom.* O matter, and impertinency mixt, Reason in Madnesse.

William the Conqueror had come before Richard III.

Why did Shakespeare not publish his plays?

It often causes surprise that Shakespeare did not arrange for his plays to be published. That he might have considered them not good enough is unthinkable. Indeed, there is clear evidence of the tremendous reception his work was given by the public. The clergyman Francis Meres in *Palladis Tamia, or Wits Treasury*, published in 1598, wrote:

'As Plautus and Seneca are accounted the best for Comedy and Tragedy among the Latines: so Shakespeare among [the] English is the most excellent in both kinds for the stage'.

The only examples of his work Shakespeare had published were *Venus and Adonis* and *The Rape of*

Shakespeare was well known among his contemporaries, who often mentioned him with admiration. None of his manuscripts has survived, however.

> As *Plautus* and *Seneca* are accounted the best for Comedy and Tragedy among the Latines : so *Shakespeare* among ỹ English is the most excellent in both kinds for the stage;

Lucrece. Meres felt the 'sweete wittie soule' of Ovid live again in these narrative poems. Of the 'sugred Sonnets', all he tells us is that they were circulated privately among Shakespeare's friends. It was not in fact until 1609 that they were published.

The theatre was not considered a truly literary genre

The theatre might provide a fair living, but this did not put it in the same rank as poetry. The text of a play was continually reworked, with a monologue added here or cut there to avoid causing offence; and there was frequent improvisation on the part of the clowns, who often strayed from the script to make the audience laugh. Hamlet goes as far as to remind the strolling players come to Elsinore to 'let those that play your clowns speak no more than is set down for them, for there be of them that will themselves laugh, to set on some quantity of barren spectators to laugh too' (Act III.ii.). Some passages were also revised after a few performances, when they had failed to produce the intended response in the audience.

The commercial art of theatre, commonly regarded as ephemeral, was in Shakespeare's eyes intended for an audience rather than for readers. The *Sonnets* stood in a different category. In their case the poet declared proudly: 'Or I shall live your epitaph to make,/ Or you survive when I in earth am rotten;/ From hence your memory death cannot take,/ Although in me each part will be forgotten./ Your name from hence immortal life shall have,/ Though I, once gone, to all the world must die..../ You still shall live, such virtue hath my pen,/ Where breath most breathes, even in the mouths of men' (sonnet no. 81).

The first pirate editions

Writing under pressure to meet public demand, Shakespeare would have found it impossible to supply a printer with a definitive text. A number of quarto volumes of his plays were nonetheless published in his lifetime. These were either poor

The title page below is from one of the 'Good Quartos', the reasonably authoritative texts that Shakespeare handed over for publication.

editions pirated by unscrupulous people seeking to profit from the success of the stage plays, or reasonably reliable texts, as in the case of *Richard II*, *Love's Labour's Lost*, *A Midsummer Night's Dream*, or *Henry IV, Part 1*. In the latter case the texts, known as the 'Good Quartos', were copied from manuscripts sold to the publisher for between £6 and £10.

In *A Midsummer Night's Dream* (Act III.i.) the people of Athens get into some bizarre situations: 'Thou art as wise as thou art beautiful', says the besotted queen of the fairies to Bottom with his ass's head. 'Not so, neither', is his reply. Left: the Man i' th' Moon, with his lantern, dog and faggot, appears at the meeting of Pyramus and Thisbe by night.

William Shakespeare
1600

Shakespeare the enigma

Who was William Shakespeare? Many critics have sought to prove that the actor Shakespeare cannot be the author of the brilliant work found in the First Folio of 1623. How could the mere son of a glover have acquired the great classical, juridical and technical knowledge revealed in his work? Where did he gain his understanding of Court circles – a man who is said to have started life holding horses at the theatre door? The philosopher, author and politician Francis Bacon, the Earls of Derby, Oxford and Essex, have all been considered as rival candidates, but none is now taken seriously. These portraits are said to be of Shakespeare: the 'Flower' portrait (facing page); the 'Ely Palace' portrait (above left); a portrait in the Folger Library (above); and a portrait attributed to Gerard Soest (left).

The company generally did this when it was short of money, and when the play in question had reached the end of its run.

Companies were anxious that copies of their plays should not proliferate, for this was the surest way of keeping the performances in their own hands. The truth was that as soon as a play was published anyone could put it on stage for his own profit. In the same way that the guilds scrupulously guarded their trade secrets, the troupes controlled the circulation of their manuscripts so as not to lose their audiences in an age when the appetite for novelty was considerable. The playwrights' manuscripts were as much part of a company's 'stock' as the costumes, sets and props. To sell them to a publisher without having exploited them to the full would have been remarkably shortsighted.

Playwrights, furthermore, viewed printers and publishers with a more than wary eye. The latter professions, based in London, belonged to the Worshipful Company of Stationers, incorporated in 1557 under an order signed by Mary Tudor.

Printing was introduced to England in 1476 by William Caxton, a former silk merchant and diplomat, who established a press at Westminster. The engraving above, dated 1620, shows a press in operation while, in the background, a typographer arranges the lead-cast letters in a printing forme. We know the names of the printers of the quartos of Shakespeare's plays. Unlike Thomas Millington, Thomas Pavier and John Danter, who published the 'Bad Quartos', Andrew Wise, Matthew Law and Cuthbert Burby only published unpirated texts.

The book trade grew up in London in the district of St Paul's, where Shakespeare lived for a time, and also in Oxford and Cambridge. Each edition numbered a few hundred, rising to a few thousand in the case of the Bible and other religious works. This engraving of a bookshop dates from 1689. The writer, or man of letters (below left), who seems to be brandishing his book like a shield, dates from c. 1616. In *Titus Andronicus* (Act IV.i.) it is thanks to a book, Ovid's *Metamorphoses*, that Lavinia is able to put her father on the trail of those who have raped her and cut off her tongue. 'TITUS: How now, Lavinia! Marcus, what means this?/ Some book there is that she desires to see./ Which is it, girl, of these? – Open them, boy. – / But thou art deeper read and better skill'd:/ Come and take choice of all my library,/ And so beguile thy sorrow, till the heavens/ Reveal the damn'd contriver of this deed.'

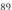

The Company had sole control of publication rights. After vetting by the official censors, the Archbishop of Canterbury and Bishop of London, every new work was duly inscribed in the Stationers' Register, which guaranteed the exclusive right to print and sell a book. The concept of copyright existed, but it was vested in the publisher, not in the author.

The 1623 folio of Shakespeare's works was printed in an edition of one thousand and sold for £1 a copy. Two hundred of them survive, fourteen of which are in perfect condition.

Elizabeth I used various symbolic images to present herself to her subjects as the Virgin Queen. She liked to be personified as Diana, classical goddess of the moon and chaste huntress; or as Astraea, goddess of justice and innocence. Like all writers of the age, Shakespeare portrayed her in terms she would find flattering.

CHAPTER 4

ELIZABETH I: MYTH AND PROPAGANDA

The Spanish Armada, which in 1588 sailed to invade Britain, ended in disaster. Queen Elizabeth was left triumphant over the Catholic forces. She is portrayed here (left) on a visit to Tilbury, at the mouth of the Thames, to speak to the troops, while the enemy ships blaze in the distance. In contrast to this image of an Amazonian queen, the miniature (right) by Isaac Oliver gives her an air of gentleness.

A symbolic bestiary, featuring notably the phoenix and the pelican, was associated to the queen. The phoenix, an icon of virginity, also expressed her uniqueness, while the pelican symbolized her devotion to her people. Portraits represent Elizabeth variously holding a rainbow, bearing the olive branch of peace, standing beside a pillar of constancy, her hand upon the globe of the earth or the heavens. She is rendered in all her majesty with emblems of the microcosm and macrocosm.

An entire mythology developed round the figure of the queen. Poets such as Sir Walter Raleigh and Sir John Davies endowed her with a range of symbolic associations which visibly influenced official paintings of processions, receptions and tournaments and even the architecture of the period. It was not unheard of for a courtier to build himself a house in the form of an 'E', the initial letter of his sovereign's name.

The royal mythology similarly marked the drama of the Elizabethan age. The comedies Shakespeare wrote between 1595 and 1600 indirectly paid tribute to the queen by making the female roles more important: Rosalind in *As You Like It*, for example, or Beatrice in *Much Ado About Nothing*. The first declares to her suitor Orlando: 'the poor world is almost six thousand years old, and in all this time there was not any man died in his own person, videlicet, in a love-cause' (Act IV.i.); and Beatrice meets Benedick's 'for truly I love none' with the retort: 'I had rather hear my dog bark at a crow than a man swear he love me' (Act I.i.).

Following the defeat of the Armada, anti-Catholic propaganda presented Elizabeth I as the great empress of the world. This anonymous 'Armada' portrait (*c.* 1588) shows her with her right hand resting on the globe. Having vanquished the forces of evil, she appears in all her glory.

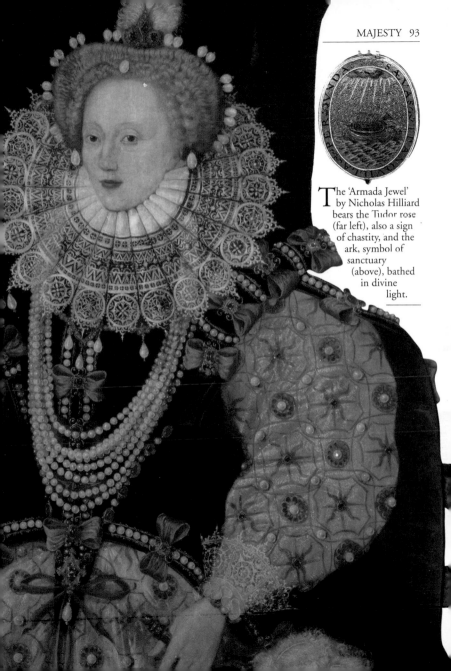

The 'Armada Jewel'
by Nicholas Hilliard
bears the Tudor rose
(far left), also a sign
of chastity, and the
ark, symbol of
sanctuary
(above), bathed
in divine
light.

'Honi soit qui mal y pense'

The portraits of Elizabeth on the preceding pages show the extent to which she was the object of a personality cult during her reign (1558–1603). Her dresses and accessories are extraordinarily lavish and richly symbolic, proclaiming the virtues and powers that she embodies. The sieve and feathers that she holds (p. 94, above) and the white flowers on her dress (p. 95) are symbols of chastity. The hand laid on her heart and the rainbow in her hand (p. 94, below) invest her with a luminous radiance. The portrait (p. 95) by Marcus Gheeraerts the Younger was probably painted for her visit to Sir Henry Lee's house, Ditchley. She is standing on the globe, with her feet pointing to Oxfordshire, where his house was located. Early in her reign the queen was presented in terms of more traditional mythology, as in this painting, where Juno, Minerva and Venus are eclipsed by the arrival of Elizabeth, a new goddess who transcends them in power, wisdom and beauty.

Images of an ideal monarchy

The festivities of the Elizabethan Court followed a well-ordered calendar, suggesting a world of uninterrupted splendour. Winter was the season of Revels, and every 17 November the queen went to Whitehall to celebrate the anniversary of her accession to the throne. Sumptuous tournaments were organized, at which her champions, courtiers like Henry Lee and Robert Ratcliffe, contended for her favours and the privilege of serving her best. There were great displays of arms, caparisoned horses, foot servants, banners flaunting coats of arms and Latin mottos composed in her honour. Next came Christmas festivities, organized by the Master of the Revels. The entertainments included music, balls, masques, and plays performed by one of the companies of the public theatres, or by the Children of Blackfriars or the Children of St Paul's.

Elizabeth was a vivacious queen with a taste for feasting and dancing, which she made an important part of Court life. In this painting of a banquet (above) she has been identified dancing the gavotte. The popularity of this pastime is evoked in *Henry V* when the French, driven back by the fierce attack of the English, turn to ironic gallantries: 'DAUPHIN: By faith and honour,/ Our madams mock at us.... BOURBON: They bid us to the English dancing schools/ And teach lavoltas high and swift corantos,/ Saying our grace is only in our heels' (*Henry V*, Act III.v.).

In summer the queen moved to the country with her entire Court, to be received with much pomp by her vassals, who vied with each other for this costly privilege. Splendid outdoor entertainments were held in her honour, in gardens and on lakes, where boating displays were followed by fireworks.

Palaces and gardens

The Elizabethan age was marked by an architectural flowering. Buildings acquired an exotic and even bizarre appearance, with a multiplication of tall gables, curious domes, façades broken by pilasters and colonnades, great casements and mullioned windows, and the tall chimneys alluded to in Shakespeare's *Henry VI, Part 1*. Neither Italian nor French, this was a peculiarly English Renaissance architecture. Inside, the rooms were many, and vast, particularly the great ceremonial halls with their elaborate timber roof beams. Floors were covered with rushes, walls with magnificent tapestries depicting pastoral and mythological scenes with floral or animal motifs.

In 1580 pleasure gardens began to come into fashion, with their clipped hedges, flowerbeds laid out in geometric or symbolic designs, mazes and fountains. The surprises and wonders that form the backdrop to a comedy such as *A Midsummer Night's Dream* were no doubt influenced by these mannerist gardens, peopled by strange statues, adorned with hedges cut in the form of heraldic beasts, chimeras and savages.

Gardeners planted their beds with flowers symbolizing purity (roses and daisies) in tribute to the Virgin Queen, foundress of a

Elizabeth turned the anniversary of her accession to the throne into a national festival. Church bells rang on the day, and the Court attended sumptuous tournaments at which knights jousted in honour of the queen. This portrait of the Earl of Sussex in armour is dated 1593.

new Golden Age. The gardens of the great country palaces and houses of Kenilworth, Theobalds and Hatfield were designed on emblematic lines, with great hedges cut to represent family coats of arms. It was in these gardens, these symbolic landscapes, that summer pageants were presented in honour of the queen. In a nature cunningly shaped by the gardener's hand, she found allegories in her own image, tributes to the mark she had made on the age.

Fireworks were a common feature of Court entertainments. They were held in the hand at the end of a long stick, as in this engraving (left) of a man dressed as a savage.

Microcosm and macrocosm

Closely linked with this symbolic vision of nature, was that of the wondrous stars and planets. The Elizabethan concept of the universe was still based on the theories of the Alexandrian astronomer Ptolemy (2nd century AD). In his system the sun and seven planets revolved in concentric spheres round a stationary earth. Below the moon was the world of mutability, above it, that of permanence. At the top lay the firmament and the fiery sphere, to which the stars were fixed like gold nails.

In fact, it was in 1543 that the Polish astronomer Nicolaus Copernicus published *De Revolutionibus Orbium Coelestium* ('On the Revolution of the Celestial Spheres'), the basis of

The curious poem below, in the form of a pyramid that reads from top to bottom, is a compliment to Queen Elizabeth.

```
                        Skie
                      Azured
                      In the
                     Assur'de
                  And better
                  And richer
                  Much greater

              Crownandempir
              After an hier
              For to aspire
              Like flame of fire
              In form of Spire

          To mount on hie
          Con-ti-nu-al-ly
          With travel and teen.
          Most gracious Queen
          Ye have made a vow
          Shews us plainly how
          Not fained but true
          To everyman s vew
          Shining cleere in you
          Of so bright an-hewe
          Even thus vertewe

        Vanish out of sight
        Till his fine top be quite
        To taper in the ayre
        Endevours soft and faire
        By his kindly nature.
        Of tall comely stature
        Like as this faire figur
```

modern astronomy; but his hypotheses were not confirmed by Johannes Kepler and Galileo Galilei until 1609 and 1610. Thus only a few learned Elizabethans knew of his theories, which formed no part of the consciousness of the age.

One of Elizabeth's finest palaces was Nonsuch in Surrey, portrayed below by Hoefnagel. It was demolished in 1680.

Astrology continued to be officially taught at university. Traditional medicine linked bodily rhythms and diseases to the motions of the seven planets, and the influence of the twelve signs of the zodiac on the various members and organs of the body. Aries, for example, ruled the head and face, Taurus the neck, Gemini the shoulders, Leo the back and heart, Cancer the chest, stomach and lungs.

Furthermore, the movements of the stars, the appearance of comets and eclipses, were believed to herald disaster and the death of princes. The human microcosm could only be understood by reference to the macrocosm of all creation. Shakespeare and his contemporaries saw nature as a unified whole which, however various its manifestations, lent itself to universal interpretation by the laws of analogy and the theory of 'signatures'.

This 16th-century engraving shows Ptolemy's system of the universe with its concentric spheres.

Elizabethan gardens

Elizabethan gardens were designed according to strict principles. The flower beds were laid out in squares or in knots, intricate patterns that could be emblematic or purely ornamental, as in these early 17th-century garden designs. The view of a garden above left is a detail of a painting by Joos de Momper, dated 1633. Flowers and vegetables were chosen for their colours and for the season of their blooming or ripening. Hedges were clipped, into geometric or animal shapes, and many stately homes had a maze in the garden. Shakespeare frequently uses the allegory of the enclosed garden, as in *Richard II* (Act III.iv.), where it serves as an image in miniature of his kingdom: 'Why should we, in the compass of a pale,/ Keep law and form and due proportion,/ Showing, as in a model, our firm estate,/ When our sea-walled garden, the whole land,/ Is full of weeds;/ her fairest flowers chok'd up,/ Her fruit trees all unprun'd, her hedges ruin'd,/ Her knots disordered, and her wholesome herbs/ Swarming with caterpillars?'

The latter were outward signs or special marks that made it possible to decipher the essence of things, of the universe; they were blazons, or hieroglyphics representing the visible face of the hidden world, enabling the wise man or seer to read the works of God in the great book of Nature. Hence the vogue for *exempla* (rhetorical moral sayings), mottos, books of emblems, compilations of all the key images and figures that determined the connections between things and relations between humans.

An entire hierarchical system thus linked the different orders of life, from minerals to angels, establishing lateral connections between plants and animals at each level or stage of the chain.

Medicine was dominated by the theories of the Greek physician Galen, who lived in the 2nd century AD. He believed there were four humours, or fluids – phlegm, blood, choler and black bile – which determined the temper of the mind and body. The melancholic humour was cold and dry, like earth, and could produce an excess of black bile; the phlegmatic humour was cold and wet, like water, and came from the kidneys or lungs; the sanguine humour was warm and humid, like air, and originated in the liver, the seat of the passions. Lastly, the choleric humour was hot and dry, like fire. Illnesses and nervous disorders were attributed to an imbalance in the humours; a just balance produced a 'good humour'. Melancholy was the

Robert Fludd, shown in this period engraving (left), had an interest in theatre and also wrote learned treatises on the relationship between the macrocosm (the universe) and the microcosm (man). Ulysses in *Troilus and Cressida* (Act I.iii.) shares his view of cosmology: 'The heavens themselves, the planets, and this centre,/ Observe degree, priority and place,/ Insisture, course, proportion, season, form,/ Office, and custom, in all line of order.... / O, when degree is shak'd,/ Which is the ladder of all high designs,/ The enterprise is sick!'

The zodiacal manuscript right is dated c. 1480.

The portrait (*c.* 1590) of a young dandy, by Isaac Oliver, conveys the world-weariness voiced by many of Shakespeare's characters, among them Jaques in *As You Like It* (Act IV.i.): 'I have neither the scholar's melancholy, which is emulation; nor the musician's, which is fantastical; nor the courtier's, which is proud; nor the soldier's, which is ambitious; nor the lawyer's, which is politic; nor the lady's, which is nice; nor the lover's, which is all these; but it is a melancholy of mine own, compounded of many simples, extracted from many objects, and, indeed, the sundry contemplation of my travels; in which my often rumination wraps me in a most humorous sadness.'

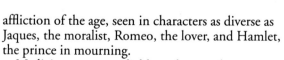

affliction of the age, seen in characters as diverse as Jaques, the moralist, Romeo, the lover, and Hamlet, the prince in mourning.

Medicines were unreliable and somewhat hazardous. They ranged from traditional pharmacopoeia, based on herbs and medicinal plants, to an assortment of drugs and ointments containing fearsome ingredients such as spider's web, hare's fur and egg shells. All such remedies proved helpless against epidemics like the plague, however, which ravaged the cities at regular intervals.

These beliefs and the ineffectiveness of medicines encouraged reliance on seers, astrologers and alchemists such as Simon Forman (1552–1611) and John Dee (1527–1608). The latter, a philosopher, mathematician, astrologer and intriguer, wrote almanacs, horoscopes and sundry predictions. He was much heeded at Court and, indeed, had no small influence on the queen.

While he did not directly serve the monarchy, Shakespeare in his dramatic works nonetheless reflected the prevalent beliefs and practices by making his characters refer to them in their speeches. Yet he never reveals himself the slave of any specific ideology or point of view, and the many contradictions that emerge in his plays are no more than the expression of an infinite diversity of opinion.

Thus in *Troilus and Cressida* (Act I.iii.), for example, Ulysses makes a long speech on the chaos that threatens when the traditional hierarchy, which he calls 'degree', is not respected (see p. 104), whereas Gloucester's bastard son Edmund in *King Lear* (Act I.ii.) mocks at astrology and its unreliable predictions: 'This is the excellent foppery of the world, that when we are sick in fortune, often the surfeits of our own behaviour, we make guilty of our disasters the sun, the moon, and stars'.

Medicine in Shakespeare's day was not far from torture. The engraving left shows the treatment for a dislocated shoulder. Deformities of birth were seen as the work of the devil, and the distinction between the real and the imagined was not always clear to learned men like the astrologer John Dee, whose portrait is above, or the surgeon Ambroise Paré. The child with a frog's head (below) illustrated one of the latter's treatises.

MR. WILLIAM SHAKESPEARES

COMEDIES, HISTORIES, & TRAGEDIES.

Publiſhed according to the True Originall Copies.

LONDON
Printed by Iſaac Iaggard, and Ed. Blount. 1623.

Elizabeth I is dead. James I succeeds. And Shakespeare loses any lingering shreds of optimism. Anxiety, uncertainty and disillusion hold sway in the theatre as Machiavellism triumphs and all opposition seems vain. Life is but a masque.

CHAPTER 5

FROM DECADENCE TO THE BAROQUE

King of Scotland since 1567, when his mother Mary Stuart was forced to abdicate, James I (1566–1625) became king of England in 1603. This portrait of him (right), dated 1610, is by John de Critz the Elder. Elizabeth's death caused no setback to Shakespeare: his career, well established by the end of her reign, forged ahead in the Jacobean era. On the left is the title page of the First Folio, 1623.

James I ascends the throne

On 24 March 1603, eve of the feast of the Annunciation and legal beginning of the year, Elizabeth I died. It was the end of an era and a dynasty. In the absence of a direct heir, the crown passed to James VI of Scotland, a Stuart and distant cousin of the queen.

James I, as he was to be known in England, soon took the Chamberlain's Men under his wing, so that they became the King's Men. The company reciprocated by putting on eleven performances between November 1604 and autumn 1605. Eager to please the sovereign, they chose seven

The funeral of the great queen took place on 28 April 1603, accompanied by a solemn procession (above and below). The crowd followed the horses draped in black, advancing with banners held high, halberds pointed to the ground. Shortly after, the plague hit London anew. Not until 1604 could James I (left) safely enter the city.

plays by Shakespeare, among which were two new works: *Measure for Measure* and *Othello*. The playwright's reputation was then at its height. Much adulated and enjoying the patronage of influential friends, he was called 'gentle Shakespeare' or, more familiarly, 'good Will'.

A new genre: 'dark comedy'

In the period between the death of Elizabeth and the coronation of James I, Shakespeare embarked on a new genre, which critics have termed the 'problem plays' or 'dark comedies'. The first of these, begun around 1601, are *Troilus and Cressida* and *All's Well That Ends Well*, ironical and troubled works; he continued in similar vein in the following years, writing *Measure for Measure, Antony and Cleopatra, Timon of Athens* and *Coriolanus,* apparently disillusioned by the uncertain political climate of the new reign.

Troilus and Cressida presents a disenchanted version of the Trojan war: the legend and splendour of ancient times are seen in an unfavourable light, as are the chivalric code of the Middle Ages and the theme of courtly love that predominates in Chaucer's *Troilus and Cressida.*

In *All's Well That Ends Well* the heroine Helena dedicates herself to the conquest of the young

At the beginning of *Henry VI, Part 1,* the Duke of Bedford exclaims: 'Hung be the heavens with black, yield day to night!/ Comets, importing change of times and states,/ Brandish your crystal tresses in the sky/ And with them scourge the bad revolting stars/ That have consented unto Henry's death!' His words would not have been inappropriate at Elizabeth's funeral.

MEASVRE
For Measure.

Which is the wiser here,
Iustice or Iniquitie?

O thou Caytiffe:
O thou Varlet!

Escalus

Elbow

Actus Secundus. Scæna Prima.

Bertram, Count of Rousillon, whom she has secretly loved since childhood; but no sooner does he marry her, under the order of the king of France, than he deserts her, and she has to use an elaborate stratagem to win him back.

Measure for Measure is set in Vienna. Duke Vincentio quits his position, leaving the puritan Angelo to enforce an ancient law punishing the crime of fornication with death, in order to cleanse the city of moral corruption. A metaphysical Machiavelli, an earthly incarnation of Providence, the duke observes the action disguised as a monk; the incorruptible Angelo falls in love with the young novice Isabella and engages in foul blackmail. Behind the ambiguous morality, behind the obvious allegory of the corruption of power, Shakespeare exposes the dark regions of the human conscience.

In *Antony and Cleopatra, Timon of Athens* and *Coriolanus*, written between 1606 and 1608, Shakespeare goes even further. He returns to the *Parallel Lives* of the Greek biographer Plutarch and to the ancient

The plays Shakespeare wrote at the start of James I's reign express doubt, disenchantment, even pessimism. One of the 'problem comedies', *Measure for Measure*, shows a distinctly corrupt Viennese society in which the virtue of the cold Isabella is (to us) as unappealing as the vice of the hypocritical Angelo, while the attitude of the duke, who perhaps represents the new sovereign, remains veiled and ambiguous, even as he works behind the scenes for the general good. *Antony and Cleopatra*, however, preserves a sense of lingering fascination and grandeur at the heart of the process of decline, which in the end triumphs and destroys the two main protagonists.

Bates · Robert Winter · Christopher Wright · John Wright · Thomas Percy · Guido Fawkes · Robert Catesby · Thomas Winter

Mediterranean world, previously featured in *Titus Andronicus* and *Julius Caesar*, but this time uses Egypt, Athens and Rome as metaphors of Jacobean society. One can see there, as if in a mirror, the quasi-imperial ambitions of James I, the internal problems of an aristocracy that is proud, isolated, split into factions and incapable of understanding the aspirations of the people. This is the background to the misjudgment that drives a hero like Coriolanus into the arms of Aufidius, Rome's greatest enemy.

Lastly, in the black fable *Timon of Athens* Shakespeare portrays a decline in values, the waning power of the nobility with the rise of self-made men

Guy Fawkes (above, 1625) and his fellow conspirators contrived a plot to blow up king and Parliament – which is where the procession below is heading. England was deeply disturbed by the Gunpowder Plot, which awakened memories of the killings under Queen Mary. Shakespeare may have known some of the plotters, from Stratford or from the Mermaid in London, a tavern popular with actors.

in the worlds of business and finance. Ruined by his friends, to whom he had in his heyday extended the most generous hospitality, Timon retreats to the desert and becomes a misanthropic hermit.

The sovereign

While he was still James VI of Scotland, James Stuart pursued scholarly studies and took an interest in the occult. Author of a number of political treatises and an enlightened lover of the arts, he was renowned both for his intelligence and for his interest in witchcraft and the supernatural. In *Daemonologie*, published in 1597, he declared his belief in evil spells and black magic. Once he was king of England, his eccentricities and despotic inclinations led him to shun public occasions and keep to his palaces. His excessive eating and drinking and predilection for beautiful young men quickly created scandal.

The Court became known for its ostentation, luxury, extravagance and love of festivities. A form of spectacle was developed there which remained popular for decades: the masque. This dramatic and musical entertainment was born of a collaboration

between the architect Inigo Jones, disciple of the Italian Andrea Palladio, who designed the sets and the playwright and poet Ben Jonson. The first of the genre, *The Masque of Blackness*, was performed at Whitehall Palace on the evening of the Epiphany in 1605. It represented the introduction to Albion of the twelve daughters of Niger, the Ethiopian river god. Moors and nymphs, Tritons and mermaids, monsters

B en Jonson, whose first comedies were put on by Shakespeare's company, increased his reputation in the reign of James I, who commissioned him to write librettos for masques to amuse the Court in the winter months. His vast classical knowledge, his reputation as a poet and his friendship, not untouched by rivalry, with Shakespeare, gave him prestige. This portrait is after Abraham van Blyenberch.

T itle page (left) of the treatise on *Daemonologie* by James VI of Scotland, the future James I.

and Nereids rose from the waves, dazzlingly arrayed, to the accompaniment of songs and dances.

The masque was in effect a huge festive show, a one-off performance that drew on the skills of technicians and poets, and involved the Court in the action. The king, queen and nobles acted and danced on the stage before concluding the occasion with a ball. In compliment to the sovereign, the plot was an expression of order and harmony, of which he was supreme guarantor.

Society and government

The splendours of the Court drew the nobility from the country to London, while the small communities previously active round the great country houses fell into decline. The old values came under threat: the tradition of hospitality and of duty to the poor slowly disappeared. The gentry were less willing to give board and lodging to the needy in return for light work, and shied away from taking in the poor over Christmas and including them in the festivities, as had been the custom. The aristocracy of the early 17th century was increasingly reluctant to assume its social responsibilities and little by little left behind the way of life that had characterized the 'Merrie England' of Good Queen Bess, as Elizabeth I was known. On the political front, James I was eager to

Ben Jonson produced some thirty masques in collaboration with Inigo Jones, who was responsible for the sets and equipment. In general these sumptuous shows were only performed once. The lavish costumes, illustrated in these two watercolours by Inigo Jones, were financed by the nobility, or even by the king or queen, who would take part in the

spectacle. The exquisite wardrobes and sets, the ingenious machinery, the play of colour, were matched by the elegant arabesques of the dance steps, which Ben Jonson termed 'the hieroglyphics of the Court'.

unite England and Scotland, and the first seeds of empire were sown. The Virginia Company of London recruited 'volunteers' to colonize the new territories, which Sir Walter Raleigh had named Virginia in honour of the Virgin Queen. The interest excited at the time by the New World is reflected in *The Tempest,* where Shakespeare dramatizes the conflict between the magus Prospero, would-be exponent of civilization, and the refractory native Caliban.

A new aesthetic

Exoticism was in fashion, and Shakespeare, like his contemporaries, was delighted to escape for a while from the decadent reality of the realm and to dream. He nevertheless transcended fantasy, using it to explore the idea of cultural difference.

Until now the unknown world had been seen in fabulous terms: the medieval *imago mundi,* as it appears on the Hereford cathedral map, featured a profusion of marvels and strange creatures: men with the heads of dogs, headless Blemmyes, with eyes and mouth set in the breast, Sciapodes, whose enormous feet served them as parasols when they lay upside-down, all were found side by side with other monsters pronounced real by the famous Greek historian Herodotus (5th century BC).

This legendary vision faded as more of the world was discovered and a more accurate and credible picture developed. While Geoffrey Chaucer, influenced by cross-currents of English, French and Italian culture, was marked by the medieval vision of the world, the

The Elizabethan period was a great age of travel. Sir Walter Raleigh (far left, in Nicholas Hilliard's miniature of *c.* 1585) set foot in Virginia in 1595. He brought back not the anticipated gold, but an unknown plant: tobacco. It became a new vice, incurring the censure of the Puritans. In 1608 Captain John Smith explored Chesapeake Bay, shown in this 17th-century map of Virginia, and brought back with him an Indian princess, Pocahontas, who became famous at Court.

Renaissance writers moved away from it, enthralled instead by the astonishing accounts of travellers to the New World. And with the flowering of Protestantism, England came to perceive the world as an infinitely varied whole, many-sided and difficult to interpret.

Such ideas run through *Othello*, in which Shakespeare daringly makes a Moor the hero of the play. Africans were unknown to the city streets of England and made an appearance only at civic occasions such as the Lord Mayor's processions in London, where the crowds were both fascinated and disturbed by their exotic looks. In the popular mind they were associated with the devil's followers or semi-pagan figures, such as

The name of Caliban, the savage slave in *The Tempest*, is a partial anagram of cannibal, an identification with the New World, whose grim culinary practices form the subject of this 16th-century engraving (below).

savages. Othello, the noble Moorish general, is the diabolic 'Other' who stirs fear and simultaneously attracts, both familiar and essentially strange.

It was after this period of great activity that Shakespeare's company took over a new playhouse. A new site, new theatrical requirements: once again the playwright broke new ground.

The private theatre at Blackfriars

Blackfriars was an old Dominican priory which had been confiscated in 1538 during the dissolution of the monasteries by Henry VIII. It was situated inside the City walls, at their western extremity, just below Ludgate. This was a liberty extending over two hectares and, because it escaped the jurisdiction of the City, highly popular with those who worked in the theatre.

The King's Men moved there in 1608. The theatre was an indoor hall, rectangular in shape and roughly 20 metres by 14. It could accommodate an audience of as many as five hundred, all seated, and each

In *The Tempest* (Act I.ii.) the young Ferdinand, son of the king of Naples, having escaped from the shipwreck and come safely to shore, hears heavenly music: 'FERDINAND: Where should this music be? I' th' air or th' earth?/ It sounds no more; and sure it waits upon/ Some god o' the island. Sitting on a bank,/ Weeping again the King my father's wreck,/ This music crept by me upon the waters,/ Allaying both their fury and my passion/ With its sweet air....

The

ARIEL: Full fathom five thy father lies;/ Of his bones are coral made;/ Those are pearls that were his eyes;/ Nothing of him that doth fade/ But doth suffer a sea-change/ Into something rich and strange.'

THE
TEMPEST.

paying a relatively high price, which ranged from sixpence to over two shillings. The company was thus able to perform in all weathers. Furthermore, it became possible to use candles to make the night scenes more realistic. Music was at the same time

The Blackfriars auditorium may perhaps have resembled the halls above: Middle Temple (left) and Charterhouse (right).

Winters Tale.

given a more important role. In the hour leading up to a performance the orchestra would play to welcome the audience, and the intervals between the acts were filled with musical entertainments, such as masques.

Most significantly, Shakespeare set out to exploit to the full the possibilities offered by the new theatre. He transcribed onto the stage a tremendous range of sensation, which combined the spectacular, the fantastic, the deeply moving. The world became a theatre, the theatre was the world, dissolving the boundaries between art and life. The stage and the role of the actor became powerful images in themselves.

In his last works, written between 1608 and 1613 – *Pericles, Cymbeline, The Winter's Tale* and *The Tempest* – Shakespeare returned to comedy. But this time his central theme was the separation and

The Winters Tale.

In *The Winter's Tale* (Act V.iii.) Paulina unveils the statue of Queen Hermione, whom everyone thinks is dead: 'PAULINA: I'll make the statue move indeed, descend/ And take you by the hand..../ Music, awake her: strike./ 'Tis time; descend; be stone no more; approach;/ Strike all that look upon with marvel..../ Bequeath to death your numbness, for from him/ Dear life redeems you.'

reuniting of parents and children. All of these plays culminate in marvellous reunions: miraculous in *Pericles*, where the young Marina rediscovers her father after escaping death at the hands of pirates and in a sordid brothel; moving in *Cymbeline*, where the old man's long-lost sons reappear, having been brought up in a cave in Wales by a faithful soldier; astonishing in *The Winter's Tale*, where Leontes re-encounters his daughter Perdita, whom he had banished at birth, believing her to be illegitimate.

This is the baroque world of illusion, which presents life as a dream: 'we are such stuff/ As dreams are made on, and our little life/ Is rounded with a sleep' are Prospero's words at the end of the masque performed to celebrate the engagement of Ferdinand and Miranda (*The Tempest*, Act IV.i.).

The Globe on fire

On 29 June 1613, while *Henry VIII* was playing at the Globe, the firing of a blank volley set fire to the thatched roof, and the theatre burnt to the ground. No one died in the blaze, but it perhaps hastened the playwright's return to New Place, Stratford.

It was there that he wrote *The Two Noble Kinsmen* with John Fletcher, the two men having earlier collaborated – a common practice at the time – on

After his theatre burnt down, if not before, Shakespeare left London for New Place, the former property of Stratford's benefactor, Sir Hugh Clopton. This imposing building had three floors and five gables, as shown in this 17th-century drawing.

Henry VIII. But in this instance it is hard to detect the hand of Shakespeare: the work is distinctly static and heavily melodramatic in its style.

'Retirement' and private affairs

All that is known of the last years of Shakespeare's life derives from documents which show that he devoted himself to his private affairs. In 1614 his name was mentioned in a controversy over the enclosure of common land in Stratford in which he had a share.

Victorian painters were much inspired by Shakespeare's works, in particular his history plays. Here G.H. Harlow represents Queen Katharine in *Henry VIII* (Act II.iv.) before the ecclesiastical tribunal convoked by the king to consider his application for divorce.

Dramatic spectacle

In the purest tradition of 19th-century history painting, the Irish artist Daniel Maclise (1806–70) represented the famous scene in which Hamlet stages *The Murder of Gonzago* before the Danish Court (*Hamlet*, Act II.ii.). Hamlet intends that in the course of the play his uncle Claudius will be exposed as the regicide that his father's ghost had proclaimed him to be: 'I have heard that guilty creatures sitting at a play/ Have by the very cunning of the scene/ Been struck so to the soul that presently/ They have proclaimed their malefactions./ For murder, though it have no tongue, will speak/ With most miraculous organ. I'll have these players/ Play something like the murder of my father/ Before mine uncle. I'll observe his looks,/ I'll tent him to the quick. If 'a do blench,/ I know my course.'

Daniel Maclise, closer to the 19th-century Italian composer Guiseppe Verdi than to Shakespeare, moves even further from Elizabethan simplicity in his painting of the banquet scene in *Macbeth*, which appears on the following pages.

Two years later, on 10 February 1616, his daughter Judith, then over thirty years old, decided to wed Thomas Quiney, a wine merchant and son of an old friend of Shakespeare. Evidence suggests the marriage was contracted to cover up a sordid affair of 'fornication', which led to the death of a Margaret Wheeler and her illegitimate child, allegedly fathered by Quiney. The resulting scandal may have damaged Shakespeare's health.

On 25 March the playwright summoned his lawyer to alter his will, taking steps to protect Judith from her perhaps unscrupulous husband. In three signed pages Shakespeare left the bulk of his property to his daughter Susanna, and his 'second best bed' to his wife Anne, a reference that continues to intrigue biographers. Possibly as a result of a trip to London, from which he returned much weakened, or after an excess of wine over dinner with his friends Michael Drayton and Ben Jonson (a story told fifty years later by the vicar of Stratford, John Ward), Shakespeare died on 23 April 1616, his fifty-second birthday.

The First Folio: 1623

Two actors in the King's Men, John Heminge and Henry Condell, gave the first collected edition of Shakespeare's plays to posterity. They were anxious both to keep Shakespeare's memory alive and to thwart the unscrupulous who were publishing works falsely under his name. The Folio volume, prepared by the printer and publisher William Jaggard and his son Isaac, was published in

Shakespeare signed all three pages of the will drawn up for him by Warwick lawyer Francis Collins. These three signatures are rare instances of his authenticated handwriting.

November 1623 and sold for £1. The preliminary pages list thirty-six of his plays (only *Pericles* and *The Two Noble Kinsmen* are omitted), divided into comedies, histories and tragedies, and also the names of the leading actors who performed in them at the Globe and Blackfriars.

Shakespeare's monument, Stratford church (far left).

The final farewell

Shakespeare's tombstone in Holy Trinity church bears this inscription, said to have been written by him:

'Good friend for Jesus sake forbear
To dig the dust enclosed here:
Blest be the man that spares these stones,
And curst be he that moves my bones.'

The stone bust of Shakespeare at Stratford (left), carved by Gerard Janssen, shows the playwright with a goose quill in his right hand, a sheet of paper in his left, looking straight ahead with a somewhat empty gaze and an air of solidity and satisfaction. But, as Ben Jonson writes in his dedicatory verse for the Folio, it is the works of his friend William that are the real monument:

'Thou art a Moniment, without a tombe,
And art alive still, while thy Booke doth live.'

'Fear no more the heat o' th' sun/ Nor the furious winter's rages;/ Thou thy worldly task hast done,/ Home art gone, and ta'en thy wages./ Golden lads and girls all must,/ As chimney-sweepers, come to dust.
'Fear no more the frown o' th' great;/ Thou art past the tyrant's stroke./ Care no more to clothe and eat;/ To thee the reed is as the oak./ The sceptre, learning, physic, must/ All follow this and come to dust.
Cymbeline, Act IV.ii.

The Workes of William Shakespeare, containing all his Comedies, Histories, and Tragedies: Truely set forth, according to their first ORIGINALL.

The Names of the Principall Actors in all these Playes.

William Shakespeare.	Samuel Gilburne.
Richard Burbadge.	Robert Armin.
John Hemmings.	William Ostler.
Augustine Phillips.	Nathan Field.
William Kempt.	John Underwood.
Thomas Poope.	Nicholas Tooley.
George Bryan.	William Ecclestone.
Henry Condell.	Joseph Taylor.
William Slye.	Robert Benfield.
Richard Cowly.	Robert Goughe.
John Lowine.	Richard Robinson.
Samuel Crosse.	John Shancke.
Alexander Cooke.	John Rice.

A CATALOGVE

of the ſeuerall Comedies, Hiſtories, and Tragedies contained in this Volume.

DOCUMENTS

Shakespeare the man

The documentary evidence of Shakespeare's personal life is meagre, but not more so than that of most men of his time and rank, and there is certainly enough to make nonsense of the idea that the man from Stratford did not write the plays. His baptism and burial are entered in the register of Stratford parish church, as are the baptisms of his children. His marriage was by special licence from the Bishop of Worcester, and this still exists.

Shakespeare and the law

There are a number of legal documents relating to Shakespeare's shares in the Globe Theatre company; his tax problems; his application for a coat of arms; and his purchase of property in London and Stratford. Of these documents, the one that sheds most light on his personality was discovered as recently as 1909.

In 1604 Shakespeare was lodging in the house of a family called Mountjoy, in Silver Street in the City of London. Christopher Mountjoy was a French Huguenot 'tire maker' (i.e. a maker of wigs and ornamental headgear). One of his apprentices was Stephen Belott, who in November 1604 married his master's daughter Mary. Eight years later, when Shakespeare had retired to Stratford, a dispute arose about how much Mountjoy had promised to give Belott as his marriage-portion. The only evidence was hearsay.

One witness remembered that:

Mr William Shakespeare tould him … that the defendant sent him, the said Mr Shakespeare, to the plaintiff about suche a marriadge to be hadd betweene them, and Shakespeare tould this deponent that the defendant tould him that yf the plaintiff would marrye the said Marye his daughter he would geve him the plaintiff a some of monney with her for a porcion in marriadge with her. And that yf he the plaintiff did not marry with her, the said Marye, and shee with the plaintiff shee should never coste him, the defendant her ffather, a groat. Whereuppon, and in regard Mr Shakespeare hadd tould them that they should have a some of monney for a porcion from the father, they weare made suer by Mr Shakespeare by geuinge there consent, and agreed to marrye, ... and did marrye.

Another stated:

that the plaintiff did requeste ... him to goe with his wyffe to Shakespe[are] to understande the truthe howe muche and what the defendant did promise [to] bestowe on his daughter in marriadge with him the plaintiff, who did soe. And askinge Shakespeare therof, he answered that he promissed yf the plaintiff would marrye with Marye his the defendantes onlye daughter, he the defendant would by his promise as he remembered geve the plaintiff with her in marriadge about the some of ffyftye poundes in money and certayne houshould stuffe.

Shakespeare was accordingly called from Stratford to testify, which he did on 11 May 1612. Not surprisingly after so long an interval, he could not remember what had been promised. What is interesting for us is that this is a unique glimpse of Shakespeare in a domestic setting (interesting, too, that he seems not to know his exact age).

William Shakespeare of Stratford upon Aven in the Countye of Warwicke gentleman of the age of xlviij yeres or thereaboutes sworne and examined the daye and yere abovesaid deposethe & sayethe
To the first interrogatory this deponent sayethe he knowethe the partyes plaintiff and deffendant and hathe know[ne] them bothe as he now remembrethe for the space of tenne yeres or thereaboutes.

To the second interrogatory this deponent sayeth he did know the complainant when he was servant with the deffendant, and that duringe the tyme of his the complainantes service with the said deffendant he the said complainant to this deponentes knowledge did well and honestly behave himselfe, but to this deponentes remembrance he hath not heard the deffendant confesse that he had gott any great profitt and comodytye by the service of the said complainant, but this deponent saithe he verely thinkethe that the said complainant was a very good and industrious servant in the said service. And more he canott depose to the said interrogatory.
To the third interrogatory this deponent sayethe that it did evydentlye appeare that the said deffendant did all the tyme of the said complainantes service with him beare and shew great good will and affeccion towardes the said complainant, and that he hath hard the deffendant and his wyefe diverse and sundry tymes saye and reporte that the said complainant was a very honest fellow: And this deponent sayethe that the said deffendant did make a mocion unto the complainant of marriadge with the said Mary in the bill mencioned beinge the said deffendantes sole chyld and daughter, and willinglye offered to performe the same yf the said complainant shold seeme to be content and well like thereof: And further this deponent sayethe that the said deffendantes wyeffe did sollicitt and entreat this deponent to move and perswade the said complainant to effect the said marriadge, and accordingly this deponent did move and perswade the complainant therunto: And more to

this interrogatorye he cannott depose.

To the ffourth interrogatory this deponent sayth that the defendant promissed to geve the said complainant a porcion … in marriadg[e] with Marye his daughter, but what certayne … porcion he rememberethe not, nor when to be payed …, nor knoweth that the defendant promissed the … plaintiff twoe hundered poundes with his daughter Marye at the tyme of his decease. But sayth that the plaintiff was dwellinge with the defendant in his house, and they had amongeste them selves manye conferences about there marriadge which afterwarde was consumated and solempnized. And more he cannott depose.

To the vth interrogatory this deponent sayth he can saye nothinge touchinge any parte or poynte of the same interrogatory, for he knoweth not what implementes and necessaries of houshould stuffe the defendant gave the plaintiff in marriadge with his daughter Marye.

Willm Shakp

Detail of a London map of the 1550s showing Silver Street, where in 1604 Shakespeare had his lodgings with a wig-maker. A character in one of Ben Jonson's plays says of another: 'All her teeth were made in the Blackfriars, both her eyebrows in the Strand, and her hair in Silver Street.'

Shakespeare the lender

No letters from Shakespeare survive, but there is one to him, from a Stratford neighbour, Richard Quiney, dated 25 October 1598, from the Bell inn in Carter Lane, asking for a loan of £30. Eighteen years later, in February 1616, the son of Richard Quiney, Thomas, married Shakespeare's daughter Judith.

To my Loveinge good ffrend & contreymann Mr Wm. Shackespere deliver thees.

Loveinge Contreyman, I am bolde of yowe as of a ffrende, craveinge yowre helpe with xxx*ll* uppon Mr Bushells & my securytee or Mr Myttons with me. Mr Rosswell is nott come to London as yeate & I have especiall cawse. Yowe shall ffrende me muche in helpeinge me out of all the debettes I owe in London, I thancke god, & muche quiet my mynde which wolde nott be indebeted. I am nowe towardes the Cowrte in hope of answer for the dispatche of my Buysenes. Yowe shall neither loase creddytt nor monney by me, the Lorde wyllinge, & nowe butt perswade yowre selfe soe as I hope & yowe shall nott need to feare butt with all hartie thanckefullenes I will holde my tyme & content yowre ffrende, & yf we Bargaine farther yowe shalbe the paiemaster yowre self. My tyme biddes me hasten to an ende & soe I committ thys [to] yowre care & hope of yowre helpe. I feare I shall nott be backe thys night ffrom the Cowrte. Haste. The Lorde be with yowe & with us all Amen. ffrom the Bell in Carter Lane the 25 October 1598. Yowres in all kyndenes Ryc. Quyney.

Shakespeare's will

By far the longest and most informative of the legal documents to have come down to us is Shakespeare's will, which was drawn up in January 1616 and amended in March. It tells us much about his circumstances and the people closest to him, but sometimes raises more questions than it answers – most notably the bequest to his wife Anne of his 'second best bed'.

In the name of God, amen! I William Shackspeare, of Stratford upon Avon in the countic of Warr. gent., in perfect health and memorie, God be praysed, doe make and ordayne this my last will and testament in manner and forme followeing, that ys to saye, First, I comend my soule into the handes of God my Creator, hoping and assuredlie beleeving, through thonelie merittes of Jesus Christe my Saviour, to be made partaker of lyfe everlastinge, and my bodye to the earth whereof yt ys made.

Item, I gyve and bequeath unto my daughter Judyth one hundred and fyftie poundes of lawfull English money, to be paied unto her in manner and forme followeing, that ys to saye, one hundred poundes in discharge of her marriage porcion within one yeare after my deceas....

Item, I gyve and bequeath unto my saied daughter Judith one hundred and fyftie poundes more, if shee or anie issue of her bodie be lyvinge att thend of three yeares next ensueing the daie of the date of this my will....

Item, I gyve and bequeath unto my saied sister Jone xx.li. and all my wearing apparrell, to be paied and delivered within one yeare after my deceas; and I doe will and devise unto her the house with thappurtenaunces in Stratford, wherein she dwelleth, for her naturall lief, under the yearelie rent of xij.d. Item, I gyve and bequeath unto her three sonns, William Harte, … Hart, and Michaell Harte, fyve poundes a peece, to be payed within one yeare after my deceas.…

Item, I gyve and bequeath unto the poore of Stratford aforesaied tenn poundes; to Mr. Thomas Combe my sword; to Thomas Russell esquier fyve poundes, and to Frauncis Collins of the borough of Warr. in the countie of Warr. gent. thirteene poundes, sixe shillinges, and eight pence, to be paied within one yeare after my deceas. Item, I gyve and bequeath to Mr. Richard Tyler thelder Hamlett Sadler xxvj.s. viij.d. to buy him a ringe; to William Raynoldes, gent., xxvj.s. viij.d. to buy him a ringe; … to my god-son William Walker xx.s. in gold; to Anthonye Nashe gent. xxvj.s. viij.d., and to Mr. John Nashe xxvj.s. viij.d. in gold; and to my fellowes, John Hemynges, Richard Burbage, and Henry Cundell, xxvj.s. viij.d. a peece to buy them ringes.

Item, I gyve, will, bequeath and devise, unto my daughter Susanna Hall, for better enabling of her to performe this my will, and towardes the performans thereof, all that capitall messuage or tenemente, with thappurtenaunces, in Stratford aforesaied, called the Newe Place, wherein I nowe dwell, and twoe messuages or tenementes with thappurtenaunces, scituat lyeing and being in Henley streete within the borough of Stratford aforesaied; and all my barnes, stables, orchardes, gardens, landes, tenementes and hereditamentes whatsoever, scituat lyeing and being, or to be had, receyved, perceyved, or taken, within the townes, hamlettes, villages, fieldes and groundes of Stratford-upon-Avon, Oldstratford, Bushopton, and Welcombe, or in anie of them in the saied countie of Warr. And alsoe all that messuage or tenemente with thappurtenaunces wherein one John Robinson dwelleth, scituat lyeing and being in the Blackfriers in London nere the Wardrobe; and all other my landes, tenementes, and hereditamentes whatsoever, To have and to hold all and singuler the saied premisses with their appurtenaunces unto the saied Susanna Hall for and during the terme of her naturall lief.…

Item, I gyve unto my wiefe my second best bed with the furniture. Item, I gyve and bequeath to my saied daughter Judith my broad silver gilt bole. All the rest of my goodes, chattels, leases, plate, jewels, and household stuffe whatsoever, after my dettes and legasies paied, and my funerall expences discharged, I gyve, devise, and bequeath to my sonne in lawe, John Hall gent., and my daughter Susanna, his wief, whom I ordaine and make executours of this my last will and testament. And I doe intreat and appoint the saied Thomas Russell esquier and Frauncis Collins gent. to be overseers hereof, and doe revoke all former wills, and publishe this to be my last will and testament. In witnes whereof I have hereunto put my hand the daie and yeare first above written.—By me William Shakespeare.

Witnes to the publishing hereof, —Fra: Collyns; Julius Shawe; John Robinson; Hamnet Sadler; Robert Whattcott.

T he last page of Shakespeare's will, with the witnesses' names at the bottom. It was drawn up by a lawyer. Only the words 'By me, William Shakespeare' are in his own handwriting.

Theatres and theatregoing

Although a visit to the theatre was one of the expeditions that every interested foreigner tried to make, there are tantalizingly few surviving accounts, and those few are tantalizingly vague.

The Dutchman Johannes de Witt, who in 1596 made the sketch of the Swan Theatre (see p. 68), has this to say about it:

There are four amphitheatres in London of notable beauty, which from their diverse signs bear diverse names. In each of them a different play is daily exhibited to the populace. The two more magnificent of these are situated to the southward beyond the Thames, and from the signs suspended before them are called the Rose and the Swan. The two others are outside the city towards the north on the highway which issues through the Episcopal Gate, called in the vernacular Bishopgate. There is also a fifth [the Bear Garden], but of dissimilar structure, devoted to the baiting of beasts, where are maintained in separate cages and enclosures many bears and dogs of stupendous size, which are kept for fighting, furnishing thereby a most delightful spectacle to men. Of all the theatres, however, the largest and the most magnificent is that one of which the sign is a swan, called in the vernacular the Swan Theatre; for it accommodates in its seats three thousand persons, and is built of a mass of flint stones (of which there is a prodigious supply in Britain), and supported by wooden columns painted in such excellent imitation of marble that it is able to deceive even the most cunning. Since its form resembles that of a Roman work, I have made a sketch of it above.

In 1599 Thomas Platter of Basel went to see Julius Caesar.

After dinner on the 21st of September, at about two o'clock, I went with my companions over the water, and in the strewn roof-house saw the tragedy of the first Emperor Julius with at least fifteen characters very well acted. At the end of the comedy they danced according to their custom with extreme elegance. Two in men's clothes and two in women's gave this peformance, in wonderful combination with each other. On another occasion, I also saw after dinner a comedy, not far from our inn, in the suburb; if I remember right, in Bishopsgate. Here they represented various nations, with whom on each occasion an Englishman fought for his daughter, and overcame them all except the German, who won the daughter in fight. He then sat down with him, and gave him and his servant strong drink, so that they both got drunk, and the servant threw his shoe at his master's head and they both fell asleep. Meanwhile the Englishman went into the tent, robbed the German of his gains, and thus he outwitted the German also. At the end they danced very elegantly both in English and in Irish fashion. And thus every day at two o'clock in the afternoon in the city of London two and sometimes three comedies are performed, at separate places, wherewith folk make merry together, and whichever does best gets the greatest audience. The places are so built, that they play on a raised platform, and every one can well see it all. There are, however, separate galleries and there one stands more comfortably and moreover can sit, but one pays more for it. Thus anyone who remains on the level standing pays only one English penny: but if he wants to sit, he is let in at a further door, and there he gives another penny. If he desires to sit on a cushion in the most

comfortable place of all, where he not only sees everything well, but can also be seen, then he gives yet another English penny at another door. And in the pauses of the comedy food and drink are carried round amongst the people, and one can thus refresh himself at his own cost.

The comedians are most expensively and elegantly apparelled, since it is customary in England, when distinguished gentlemen or knights die, for nearly the finest of their clothes to be made over and given to their servants, and as it is not proper for them to wear such clothes but only to imitate them, they give them to the comedians to purchase for a small sum.

What they can thus produce daily by way of mirth in the comedies, every one knows well, who has happened to see them acting or playing....

With such and many other pastimes besides the English spend their time; in the comedies they learn what is going on in other lands, and this happens without alarm, husband and wife together in a familiar place, since for the most part the English do not much use to travel, but are content ever to learn of foreign matters at home, and ever to take their pastime.

On 29 June 1613 the Globe Theatre burned down during a performance of Henry VIII. The Survey of London *by John Stow (continued by Edmond Howes) has this account:*

Upon S. Peters day last, the play-house or Theater, called the Globe, upon the Banck-side near London, by negligent discharging of a peal of ordinance, close to the south-side thereof, the thatch took fire, and the wind sodainly disperst the flame round about, and in a very short space the whole building was quite consumed, and no man hurt; the house being filled with people to behold the play, viz. of Henry the Eighth. And the next spring it was new builded in far fairer manner than before.

A letter from Sir Henry Wotton to his nephew goes into more detail.

Now to let matters of state sleep, I will entertain you at the present with what has happened this week at the Bank's side. The King's players had a new play, called *All is True*, representing some principal pieces of the reign of Henry VIII, which was set forth with many extraordinary circumstances of pomp and majesty, even to the matting of the stage; the Knights of the Order with their Georges and garters, the Guards with their embroidered coats, and the like: sufficient in truth within a while to make greatness very familiar, if not ridiculous. Now, King Henry making a masque at the Cardinal Wolsey's house, and certain chambers being shot off at his entry, some of the paper, or other stuff, wherewith one of them was stopped, did light on the thatch, where being thought at first but an idle smoke, and their eyes more attentive to the show, it kindled inwardly, and ran round like a train, consuming within less than an hour the whole house to the very grounds. This was the fatal period of that virtuous fabric, wherein yet nothing did perish but wood and straw, and a few forsaken cloaks; only one man had his breeches set on fire, that would perhaps have broiled him, if he had not by the benefit of a provident wit put it out with bottle ale.

Letter of 1 July 1613

The Rose Theatre

Until recently no vestige of an Elizabethan theatre was thought to exist. But in 1988 workmen excavating for a new office block near Southwark Bridge came upon the foundations of the Rose Theatre. Built about 1587, the Rose was owned and managed by Burbage's rival, Philip Henslowe, and it is therefore unlikely that any of Shakespeare's plays were performed there (except possibly Henry VI*). The physical remains are nevertheless of outstanding value in providing information about the size, shape and planning of an Elizabethan playhouse; see reconstruction on p. 69.*

It was an irregular polygon with the entrance on the south and the stage on the north. The gap between the inner and outer walls gives the width of the galleries (3.5 m). The central space sloped down to the stage – a fact unsuspected by theatre historians hitherto. The stage area itself was fragmentary, but gave evidence of having been enlarged by being extended backwards, a development confirmed by Henslowe's own financial accounts for 1592.

The site has been carefully preserved, but is now immured in the basement of the office block.

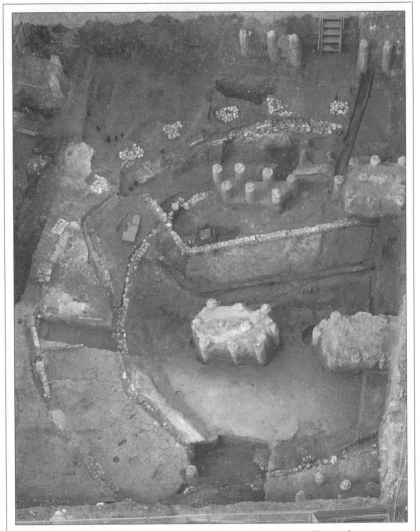

The foundations of the Rose Theatre, as they were revealed in 1988. The two large concrete slabs and the posts at the top of the picture belong to modern buildings and should be ignored. The main features (see key on left) are, A: outer wall; B: inner wall of gallery; C: standing space for spectators; D: original position of stage; E: later position of stage after the theatre was extended to the north (top).

Shakespeare the author

The First Folio of 1623 divided Shakespeare's plays into histories, comedies and tragedies. The histories, or historical dramas, consist of ten works; the comedies fall into four distinct categories: the early comedies, the romantic comedies, the problem comedies and those of the last period, also termed 'romances' or tragicomedies. People further distinguish the Roman tragedies, namely Julius Caesar, Antony and Cleopatra *and* Coriolanus, *the tragedies of passion, such as* Romeo and Juliet *and* Othello, *the revenge tragedies,* Titus Andronicus *and* Hamlet, *and finally those based on historical chronicles,* King Lear *and* Macbeth.

The diversity of Shakespeare's theatre

With the exception of two isolated works, *King John* (1596–7) and *Henry VIII* (1612–3), the history plays consist essentially of two tetralogies which form a sequence of eight plays. In the First Folio they are presented in chronological order rather than in order of composition.

The subject matter of the histories is drawn from the chronicles of the historians John Hall and Raphael Holinshed. They illustrate the tribulations of Fortune, whose fickle wheel casts princes into the depths after raising them to the heights, and also the diverse manifestations of divine providence.

These works portray the destiny of kings, a destiny often unhappy or tragic. The crown, an object of fascination, seems to crush its wearer, who is forced to confront treachery, masked by flattery, or open rebellion. The sovereign, despite his aura of divine legitimacy, lives under threat of usurpation. He must wield his authority to kill any stirrings of rebellion in their infancy. In some instances the king proves incompetent, or his right to rule is challenged – as in the case of Richard II, blinded by parasitic counsellors, favourites who destroy the garden symbolic of his kingdom – while in others he is a villain, a monster, on the lines of Richard III, who inflicts an age of bloody tyranny on his people. The series of plays about history and royal reigns illustrates the theme of the monarch's grandeur and destitution: stripped of the trappings and symbols of his power, he is revealed as a man like any other, weak and full of anguish in the face of death. These histories, in which politics are as much an expression of rivalries between families and clans as of human ambition and *hubris*, resound with the clash of battle and are rendered on stage as terrible martial displays disintegrating into breathless combat.

The comedies are an important part of Shakespeare's work; he wrote them throughout his career, and they account for half of his plays. The first comedies were written between the years 1593 and 1596 and consist of five main titles: *The Comedy of Errors, The Taming of the Shrew, The Two Gentlemen of Verona, Love's Labour's Lost* and *A Midsummer Night's Dream.* These plays are all very different from each other and present different types of humour in their handling of the themes of illusion and mistaken identity, as well as rivalry in love and the war between the sexes.

The comedies of the mature period, also known as the romantic comedies, were all written in the five following years, between 1596 and 1600, and include *The Merchant of Venice, Much Ado About Nothing, As You Like It* and *Twelfth Night. The Merry Wives of Windsor*, in a category apart, was written in two or three weeks in response to the queen's wish to see Falstaff in a romantic intrigue.

In the romantic comedies it is love that forms the principal theme; love is the primary concern of the young protagonists, whose impulses are thwarted by parental opposition or the intrigues of mean-minded individuals. However, after a period of trials that takes them into a strange and, at the same time, restorative environment (the forest near Athens in *A Midsummer Night's Dream*, Portia's palace at Belmont in *The Merchant of Venice*), the pains of love are brought to an end, resolved by a wedding feast or multiple marriages.

Shakespeare then wrote darker comedies, known as the problem comedies because of their more philosophical tone or comparatively disturbing character; for example, *Troilus and Cressida*, a play sometimes classed among the tragedies, *All's Well That Ends Well* and *Measure for Measure.*

Strangely, Shakespeare wrote only a few tragedies at the beginning of his career. Three years after *Titus Andronicus*, a play inspired by Seneca and the mythology of Ovid – and once thought to be impossible to stage because of its serried atrocities and scenes of mutilation and cannibalism – he wrote *Romeo and Juliet*. This is a tragedy of passion, but even more of fate, for the death of the young couple is brought about by a series of unhappy coincidences rather than by evil or malevolent characters; until the very end one hopes that the fatal outcome will be avoided. The play is further identified as an early work by its stirring lyricism, the intensity of the images and the pronounced contrasts between night and day, youth and age, love and death.

Easier to categorize are the Roman plays, *Julius Caesar, Antony and Cleopatra* and *Coriolanus*, which follow in the footsteps of the historical plays of the first period. This time Shakespeare finds his sources in Plutarch's *Parallel Lives*, translated in 1579 by Thomas North, rather than in Holinshed's *Chronicles. Julius Caesar* and *Coriolanus* are as much political dramas as cruel confrontations between the envisioned ideal (Brutus) or ambition (Coriolanus) and reality; *Antony and Cleopatra* is first and foremost a tragedy of sexual passion.

But it is above all the four great tragedies, *Hamlet, Othello, King Lear* and *Macbeth*, that characterize the second period of Shakespeare's career, which began when his troupe moved to the Globe Theatre. *Hamlet* is in the genre of the revenge tragedy originated by Thomas Kyd in *The Spanish Tragedy* (1592) and probably also in another, now lost, pre-*Hamlet*, play which would have served Shakespeare as a model. However, *Hamlet* is also a problem play, its hero questioning himself as to the reality of his father's ghost and, unlike other avengers, procrastinating in the execution of the task with which the spectre has charged him. A political tragedy, a philosophical drama, a contemplation on the theatre by the theatre (in the scenes featuring actors and in the play within the play), this tragedy is Shakespeare's best known, and in its richness and complexity it holds a central place in his work.

Othello is a domestic tragedy, or a comedy that ends badly under the imperial dictates of jealousy. This is a tragedy of illusion, in which the relationship between appearance and reality is distorted by the cunning of an evil manipulator and the credulity of a foreigner who believes in the power of words.

King Lear, the plot of which is drawn from English historical legend, is also a tale of illusion, of the blindness of a king mistreated by two of his daughters, who flatter him with fine words. Lear makes the mistake of dividing his kingdom between them while banishing the third daughter; she loves him most but refuses to take part in the masquerade of declarations of affection demanded by the old king. It takes the trials of madness, destitution, confrontation with the fool and with Edgar, disguised as a beggar and also banished by his own father, to bring Lear to the point of understanding the frailty of the human condition and the enormity of his own error.

Macbeth marks a forceful return to the supernatural, glimpsed in the ghostly apparitions of *Hamlet*, with the incantations and machinations of the three Weird Sisters, who come to tempt the valiant warrior in the wake of battle and sow doubt and ambition in his mind. Driven to regicide by his wife's greed for power, he becomes a bloody tyrant, ready to make every compromise with the forces of evil to preserve his power. A metaphysical drama as much as a political tragedy, *Macbeth* translates the conflict of good and evil into cosmic terms and, in the power of its language, provides a terrifying vision of the empire of darkness and its business of destroying innocence and the springs of life.

In the last stage of his career Shakespeare concentrated on a relatively new type of play known as a romance, no doubt written to satisfy the public taste for sentiment and to exploit the marvellous stage effects made possible by the acquisition of the private theatre at Blackfriars. These are the works written between 1608 and 1613, namely *Pericles, Cymbeline, The Winter's Tale, The Tempest* and *The Two Noble Kinsmen*, leaving aside the play *Henry VIII*, which is closer in style to the historical dramas than to the last comedies.

François Laroque

The mystery of 'Mr W.H.'

Shakespeare's Sonnets *were published in 1609, though not by him. Most of them had been written ten or even twenty years earlier. The first 127 are addressed to a beautiful young man whom the poet urges to marry and beget a child. Another 27 concern a 'dark lady' who is the poet's mistress. In lieu of a dedication, the following enigmatic note appears on the first page. Although clearly not by Shakespeare ('T.T.' is the printer, Thomas Thorpe), it has given rise to more speculation than anything he ever wrote. Who is 'Mr W.H.'? The once favourite candidate was Henry Wriothesley ('H.W.'); there have been many other suggestions and will doubtless be many more.*

TO.THE.ONLIE.BEGETTER.OF.
THESE.INSVING.SONNETS.
Mr.W.H. ALL.HAPPINESSE.
AND.THAT.ETERNITIE.
PROMISED.

BY.

OVR.EVER-LIVING.POET.

WISHETH.

THE.WELL-WISHING.
ADVENTVRER.IN.
SETTING.
FORTH.

T. T.

The enigmatic dedication to Shakespeare's *Sonnets*, 1609.

The early works

Shakespeare was a poet before he was a playwright. Venus and Adonis *was published in 1593,* The Rape of Lucrece *in 1594. These poems are the only works that Shakespeare seems to have published himself. Both contain fulsome dedications to Henry Wriothesley, Earl of Southampton, to whom the young poet was clearly looking as a patron. Disappointingly, they are the only statements that we have by Shakespeare on any of his works. How close the relationship was, or what benefits Southampton's patronage brought, is unknown (a later story relates that he lent Shakespeare £1000, which seems unlikely). The dedication to* Venus and Adonis *reads as follows:*

RIGHT HONOURABLE
I know not how I shall offend in dedicating my unpolished lines to your lordship, nor how the world will censure me for choosing so strong a prop to support so weak a burden: only, if your honour seem but pleased, I account myself highly praised, and vow to take advantage of all idle hours, till I have honoured you with some graver labour. But if the first heir of my invention prove deformed, I shall be sorry it had so noble a godfather, and never after ear so barren a land, for fear it yield me still so bad a harvest. I leave it to your honourable survey, and your honour to your heart's content; which I wish may always answer your own wish, and the world's hopeful expectation.

Your honour's in all duty,
WILLIAM SHAKESPEARE

TO THE RIGHT
HONOVRABLE, HENRY
VVriothesley, Earle of Southampton,
and Baron of Titchfield.

HE loue I dedicate to your
Lordship is without end:wher-
of this Pamphlet without beginning is but a superfluous
Moity. The warrant I haue of
your Honourable disposition,
not the worth of my vntutord
Lines makes it assured of acceptance. VVhat I haue
done is yours, what I haue to doe is yours, being
part in all I haue, deuoted yours . VVere my worth
greater, my duety would shew greater, meane time,
as it is,it is bound to your Lordship; To whom I wish
long life still lengthned with all happinesse.

Your Lordships in all duety.

William Shakespeare.

Dedication page of *The Rape of Lucrece*, 1594.

A Shakespeare manuscript?

Around 1592–3 the playwrights Anthony Munday and Henry Chettle produced the script of a play called Sir Thomas More and submitted it to the Queen's Master of the Revels, Edmund Tilney, whose job it was to license plays for public performance. Sir Thomas More contained a number of problems, one of which was a scene showing Londoners rioting against foreign merchants in the City and being pacified by More (an incident that occurred in 1517). Tilney was nervous, because a new wave of xenophobic feeling was at that moment disturbing the City. He wrote: 'Leave out the insurrection wholly, with the cause thereof, and begin with Sir Thomas More at the Mayor's sessions – with a report afterwards of his good service done being Sheriff of London upon a mutiny against the Lombards – only by a short report and not otherwise – at your own perils. E. Tilney.'

This would have meant virtually sabotaging the play, and what seems to have happened is that Munday and Chettle called on the services of another playwright, who rewrote the whole scene, providing More with a powerful speech recommending law and order. Even this, however, failed to win approval for the play; it was never acted or printed, and the manuscript was left to moulder, eventually finding its way into the collection of the British Library, London.

It is in a chaotic and sometimes illegible state, in at least five different handwritings, but what has attracted the interest of scholars is the three pages containing the revised scene of More and the rioters. They are written in a different hand from the rest, and the style is in many obvious ways superior. Was Shakespeare the author, and do we have here a unique example of a manuscript in his own autograph? The arguments – on style, content, spelling, handwriting – are strong, but the final answer can never be known.

The content of More's speech, arguing for peace, compromise and submission to lawful authority, is in tune with similar speeches in Shakespeare; the style is direct but rich in imagery; and even the spelling accords with what is known (or can be deduced) of Shakespeare's spelling – most notably 'scilens' for 'silence'. The question will no doubt always remain open, except in the unlikely event that another manuscript turns up. In the extract shown opposite More argues with the crowd, appealing to their sense of justice, and asking them to put themselves in the place of the foreigners whom they want to drive out. He promises mercy from the king, but in the event that promise cannot be kept.

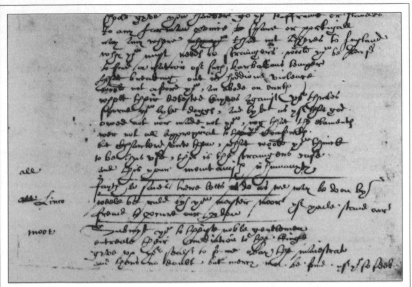

Part of the manuscript of *Sir Thomas More*, with the same passage in modern spelling.

To any German province, Spain or Portugal,
Nay, anywhere that not adheres to England
Why, you must needs be strangers. Would you be pleased
To find a nation of such barbarous temper,
That, breaking out in hideous violence,
Would not afford you an abode on earth,
Whet their detested knives against your throats,
Spurn you like dogs and like as if that God
Owed not nor made not you, nor that the elements
Were not all appropriate to your comforts
But chartered unto them? What would you think
To be thus used? This is the strangers' case,
And this your montanish inhumanity.
All. Faith! He says true; let's do as we may be done by.
Lincoln. We'll be ruled by you, Master More, if you'll
stand our friend to procure our pardon.
More. Submit you to these noble gentlemen,
Entreat their mediation to the King,
Give up yourself to form, obey the Magistrate,
And there's no doubt but mercy may be found
If you so seek it.

Public opinion

The first public mention of Shakespeare as a playwright is a hostile one – in Robert Greene's Groatsworth of Wit *of 1592 (see pp. 47–8). Greene addresses three other dramatists (Christopher Marlowe and probably George Peele and Thomas Nashe) to warn them against an ignorant newcomer, not educated at a university, who is shouldering his way into the profession.*

Base minded men al three of you, if by my miserie ye be not warned; for unto none of you, like me, sought those burres to cleave; those puppits, I meane, that speake from our mouths, those anticks garnisht in our colours. Is it not strange that I, to whom they al have beene beholding, is it not like that you to whome they all have beene beholding, shall, were ye in that case that I am now, be both at once of them forsaken? Yes, trust them not; for there is an upstart crow, beautified with our feathers, that, with his *Tygers heart wrapt in a Players hide*, supposes he is as well able to bumbast out a blanke verse as the best of you; and being an absolute *Johannes Factotum*, is in his owne conceit the onely Shakescene in a countrie. O that I might intreate your rare wits to be imployed in more profitable courses, and let those apes imitate your past excellence, and never more acquaint them with your admired inventions! I know the best husband of you all will never prove an usurer, and the kindest of them all wil never proove a kinde nurse; yet, whilst you may, seeke you better maisters, for it is pittie men of such rare wits should be subject to the pleasures of such rude groomes.

More interesting than this mean-spirited attack by the dying Greene is the response that it provoked from another author, Henry Chettle, who had seen Groatsworth of Wit *through the press. In a statement of his own, included in another pamphlet, he tells us that two people had taken offence at Greene's words. One of them was probably Marlowe, who had been called an atheist and a disciple of Machiavelli; the other was clearly Shakespeare. The first, says Chettle, he cares not if he never meets; the second had previously been unknown to him, but upon looking into the matter he feels obliged to apologize.*

About three moneths since died M. Robert Greene, leaving many papers in sundry booksellers hands, among other his Groatsworth of Wit, in which a letter, written to divers play-makers, is offensively by one or two of them taken; and because on the dead they cannot be avenged, they wilfully forge in their conceites a living author; and after tossing it two and fro, no remedy but it must light on me. How I have all the time of my conversing in printing hindred the bitter inveying against schollers, it hath been very well knowne; and how in that I dealt, I can sufficiently proove. With neither of them that take offence was I acquainted, and with one of them I care not if I never be. The other, whome at that time I did not so much spare as since I wish I had, for that, as I have moderated the heate of living writers, and might have usde my owne discretion, – especially in such a case, the author beeing dead, – that I did not I am as sory as if the originall fault had beene my fault, because myselfe have seene his demeanor no lesse civill, than he exelent in the qualitie he professes; – besides, divers of worship have reported his uprightnes of dealing, which argues his honesty, and his facetious grace in writting, that aprooves his art.

This is a curious incident. Shakespeare evidently had powerful friends to protest on his behalf. Who were they?

In 1598 a book by a scholarly connoisseur called Francis Meres, Wits Treasury, contains a 'comparative discourse of our English Poets with the Greek, Latin and Italian poets', in the course of which he lists what were evidently regarded as Shakespeare's best plays up to that time.

As Plautus and Seneca are accounted the best for comedy and tragedy among the Latines, so Shakespeare among the English is the most excellent in both kinds for the stage; for comedy, witnes his Gentlemen of Verona, his Errors, his Love labors lost, his Love labours wonne, his Midsummers night dreame, and his Merchant of Venice; for tragedy, his Richard the 2, Richard the 3, Henry the 4, King John, Titus Andronicus and his Romeo and Juliet. As Epius Stolo said that the Muses would speake with Plautus tongue, if they would speak Latin; so I say that the Muses would speak with Shakespeare's fine filed phrase, if they would speake English.

Friends and foes

When John Heminge and Henry Condell collected Shakespeare's plays to be published in the First Folio of 1623, they added their tribute to him and to the ease with which he wrote.

It had bene a thing, we confesse, worthie to have bene wished, that the Author himselfe had liv'd to have set forth, and overseen his owne writings; But since it hath been ordain'd otherwise, and he by death departed from that right, we pray you do not envie his Friends, the office of their care, and paine, to have collected & publish'd them, and so to have publish'd them, as where (before) you were abus'd with diverse stolne, and surreptitious copies, maimed, and deformed by the frauds and stealthes of iniurious impostors, that expos'd them: even those, are now offer'd to your view cur'd, and perfect of their limbes; and all the rest, absolute in their numbers, as he conceived them. Who, as he was a happie imitator of Nature, was a most gentle expresser of it. His mind and hand went together: And what he thought, he uttered with that easiness, that wee have scarce received from him a blot in his papers. But it is not our province, who onely gather his works, and give them you, to praise him. It is yours that reade him. And there we hope, to your divers capacities, you will finde enough, both to draw, and hold you: for his wit can no more lie hid, then it could be lost. Reade him, therefore; and againe, and againe: And if then you doe not like him, surely you are in some manifest danger, not to understand him. And so we leave you to other of his Friends, whom if you need, can bee your guides: if you neede them not, you can leade your selves, and others. And such Readers we wish him.

Ben Jonson's admiration for Shakespeare was warm but not uncritical. On reading this testimony of Heminge and Condell he could not withhold a certain scorn.

I *remember*, the Players have often mentioned it as an honour to *Shakespeare*, that in his writing, (whatsoever he penn'd) hee never blotted out line. My answer hath beene, would he had blotted a thousand. Which they thought a malevolent speech. I had not told posterity this, but for their ignorance, who choose that circumstance to commend their friend by, wherein he most faulted. And to justifie mine owne candor, (for I lov'd the man, and doe honour his memory (on this side Idolatry) as much as any.) Hee was (indeed) honest, and of an open, and free nature: had an excellent *Phantsie*; brave notions, and gentle expressions: wherein hee flow'd with that facility, that sometime it was necessary he should be stop'd: *Sufflaminandus erat*; as *Augustus* said of *Haterius*. His wit was in his owne power; would the rule of it had beene so too. Many times hee fell into those things, could not escape laughter: As when hee said in the person of *Caesar*, one speaking to him; *Caesar thou dost me wrong*. Hee replyed: *Caesar did never wrong, but with just cause* and such like: which were ridiculous. But hee redeemed his vices, with his vertues. There was ever more in him to be praysed, then to be pardoned.

This was not the first time that Jonson had sniped at Shakespeare. When he visited the Scottish poet William Drummond in 1618 he had this to say, among other things:

Sheakspear in a play brought in a number of men saying they had suffered Shipwrack in Bohemia, wher ther is no Sea neer by some 100 Miles.

Playgoers' testimony

Thousands of Londoners went to see Shakespeare's plays. Very few of them recorded their impressions. In February 1602 a law student called John Manningham went to see a play – Twelfth Night *– performed in Middle Temple Hall, and wrote this in his diary:*

At our feast wee had a play called Twelve night or what you will, much like the commedy of errors or Menechmi in plautus but most like and neere to that in Italian called Inganni a good practise in it to make the steward beleeve his Lady widdowe was in Love wth him by counterfayting a lettr as from his Lady in generall tearmes telling him what shee liked best in him and prescribing his gesture in smiling his apparaile etc. And then when he came to practise making him beleeve they tooke him to be mad.

A more assiduous theatregoer was Simon Forman, doctor, magician and amateur psychiatrist. In April 1611 (he put 1610 by mistake) he went to see Macbeth *and left a detailed and thoughtful description of it.*

In Mackbeth at the Glob, 1610, the 20 of Aprill [Saturday], ther was to be observed, firste, howe Mackbeth and Bancko, 2 noble men of Scotland, Ridinge thorowe a wod, the[r] stode before them 3 women feiries or Nimphes, And saluted Mackbeth, sayinge, 3 tyms unto him, haille Mackbeth, king of Codon; for thou shalt be a kinge, but shalt beget No kinges, etc. Then said Bancko, What all to Mackbeth And nothing to me.

Yes, said the nimphes, haille to thee Bancko, thou shalt beget kinges, yet be no kinge. And so they departed & cam to the Courte of Scotland to Dunkin king of Scotes, and yt was in the dais of Edward the Confessor. And Dunkin bad them both kindly wellcome, And made Mackbeth forth with Prince of Northumberland, and sent him hom to his own castell, and appointed Mackbeth to provid for him, for he would sup with him the next dai at night, & did soe. And Mackebeth contrived to kill Dunkin, & thorowe the persuasion of his wife did that night Murder the kinge in his owne Castell, beinge his guest. And ther were many prodigies seen that night & the dai before. And when Mack Beth had murdred the kinge, the blod on his handes could not be washed of by Any meanes, nor from his wives handes, which handled the bloddi daggers in hiding them, By which means they became both moch amazed & Affronted. The murder being knowen, Dunkins 2 sonns fled, the on to England, the [other to] Walles, to save them selves, they being fled, they were supposed guilty of the murder of their father, which was nothinge so. Then was Mackbeth crowned kinge, and then he for feare of Banko, his old companion, that he should beget kinges but be no kinge him selfe, he contrived the death of Banko, and caused him to be Murdred on the way as he Rode. The next night, beinge at supper with his noble men whom he had bid to a feaste to the which also Banco should have com, he began to speake of Noble Banco, and to wish that he wer ther. And as he thus did, standing up to drincke a Carouse to him, the ghoste of Banco came and sate down in his cheier

behind him. And he turninge About to sit down Again sawe the goste of Banco, which fronted him so, that he fell into a great passion of fear and fury, Utterynge many wordes about his murder, by which, when they hard that Banco was Murdred they Suspected Mackbet.

Then MackDove fled to England to the kinges sonn, And soe they Raised an Army, And cam into Scotland, and at Dunston Anyse overthrue Mackbet. In the meantyme whille Macdovee was in England, Mackbet slewe Mackdoves wife & children, and after in the battelle Macdove slewe Mackbet.

Observe Also howe Mackbetes quen did Rise in the night in her slepe, & walke and talked and confessed all, & the docter noted her wordes.

Forman saw three other Shakespeare plays in the course of the year – Cymbeline, Richard II *and* The Winter's Tale – *and left equally circumstantial accounts of them.*

MR ANDERSON, AS MACBETH.
London, Published by J.A[...]

Shakespeare studies

Shakespeare criticism began in England with the work of the neo-classical writers Alexander Pope and Samuel Johnson, who won credence for the idea that the playwright's genius allowed him to rise above the rules drawn up by Aristotle in his Poetics — *an idea to which Voltaire, who made Shakespeare known on the European continent, did not subscribe.*

German men of letters Johann Wolfgang von Goethe, Friedrich von Schlegel and Johann Ludwig Tieck waxed enthusiastic over Shakespeare's work. In England William Wordsworth expressed the belief that the *Sonnets* held the key to Shakespeare's heart. John Keats identified in a letter what he termed his 'negative capability': 'that is, when a man is capable of being in uncertainties, mysteries, doubts, without any irritable reaching after fact and reason'. And Samuel Taylor Coleridge wrote numerous essays on the plays, emphasizing the often remarkable qualities of his female characters. For him, Shakespeare was as mysterious and elusive as Proteus, god of the sea and metamorphosis. In France, Stendhal expressed great admiration for Shakespeare, whom he saw as the master of prose drama, while Victor Hugo, whose plays show the undeniable influence of the great Elizabethan, was even more strongly impressed by him. Hugo acclaimed the universality of Shakespeare's genius in his work *William Shakespeare*, written in 1864.

In the 20th century criticism was dominated by A.C. Bradley, who in 1904 published a series of lectures devoted to the psychological study of the main characters in the great tragedies (*Hamlet, Othello, King Lear* and *Macbeth*) under the title *Shakespearean Tragedy*. After the war a Cambridge professor, L.C. Knights, wrote ironically about the tendency of critics to treat fictitious characters as if they were entirely real human beings in a famous article published in 1933, entitled *How Many Children had Lady Macbeth?* He articulated the idea that Shakespeare was, first and foremost, a

To the Reader.

This Figure, that thou here seest put,
  It was for gentle Shakespeare cut:
Wherein the Grauer had a strife
  with Nature, to out-doo the life:
O, could he but haue drawne his wit
  As well in brasse, as he hath hit
His face; the Print would then surpasse
  All, that was euer writ in brasse.
But, since he cannot, Reader, looke
  Not on his Picture, but his Booke.

K*ing Lear Weeping over the Body of Cordelia*, 18th-century engraving after James Barry.

dramatic poet and that his work had to be analysed through its images and words. This aspect of his writing then drew greater critical attention, specifically in Caroline Spurgeon's book *Shakespeare's Imagery, and What It Tells Us* (1935) and the many essays published by George Wilson Knight (1933).

The trend in the 1930s and 1940s was to return to the study of historical background, for example in the work of E.M.W. Tillyard, *The Elizabethan World Picture* (1943). In his eyes, Shakespeare was complying with Tudor ideology when he wrote his historical dramas, presenting the Duke of Richmond (Henry VII), for example, in his official light as providential saviour of an English nation torn apart by the horrors of civil war. These theories are heavily disputed today, particularly by those who think in terms of cultural materialism, and see Shakespeare, contrarily, as a writer who sympathized with the oppressed (women and the poor) and whose superficial allegiances masked criticism of the mechanisms of power.

In France Shakespeare criticism found its expression in the work of Henri Fluchère, *Shakespeare dramaturge élisabéthain* ('Shakespeare, Elizabethan Dramatist'), published in 1947. A disciple of the Cambridge school led by L.C. Knights and F.R. Leavis, and influenced by T.S. Eliot's essays, Fluchère concentrated on analysis of the poetic quality of Shakespeare's work rather than of the author's life and the psychology of his characters: 'It is only the man's work and not his actions and behaviour that concern us.... The man and the mystery about him have relegated his work to second place for too long'. Meanwhile, in England, Allardyce Nicoll and Glynne Wickham studied the organization of the theatres and companies; Kenneth Muir and Geoffrey Bullough did research on the sources of the plays which helped extend the traditional approach to Shakespeare's work and gave access to new information, both historical and iconographic, throwing light on Shakespeare's contribution to the theatre of his time.

The Cold War period and the rise of existentialism and Marxism gave birth to materialist analyses of Shakespeare's drama, such as *Shakespeare Our Contemporary* (1964) by the Polish writer Jan Kott. His ideas greatly influenced the productions of the 1960s, in particular those of Peter Brook, who drew on them considerably. In Kott's eyes there were no good or bad kings, only the implacable steamroller of history crushing individuals like an inhuman machine. This materialist critical approach, influenced predominantly by Karl Marx and Bertolt Brecht, developed significantly with the work of Robert Weimann, *Shakespeare and Popular Tradition in the Theatre*, published in German in 1967 and in English translation in 1978, inviting comparison with *Rabelais and Popular Culture in the Middle Ages and the Renaissance* (1970) by the Russian Mikhail Bakhtin.

Psychoanalysts have also taken a great interest in Shakespeare's writing, starting with Sigmund Freud himself, who numbered the playwright's works among his bedside books, often referred to him, and even wrote important articles on his plays. Freud's disciple Ernest Jones explained Hamlet's

Lady Macbeth steeling herself for the murder of Duncan, a late 18th-century engraving after Richard Westall.

puzzling hesitation in enacting the vengeance demanded by his dead father in terms of the Oedipus complex: Hamlet hated Claudius and at the same time envied him for occupying the place by Queen Gertrude's side that he himself secretly desired. In the aftermath of this now classic study, essays and articles from the psychoanalytic standpoint have multiplied. Among the more recent are Jacques Lacan's articles on *Hamlet*, Bernard Sichère's *Le Nom de Shakespeare* ('The Name of Shakespeare') and *Avec Shakespeare* ('With Shakespeare') by the psychoanalyst Daniel Sibony.

In the last fifteen years Shakespeare criticism has been enlivened, not to say disturbed, by a variety of schools of thought: feminism, Deconstructionism (notably the theories of the French philosopher Jacques Derrida) and the New Historicism. The latter movement, spearheaded by Stephen Greenblatt, author of *Renaissance Self-Fashioning* (1980), aims to situate Shakespeare's work in its historical context, in relation to his contemporaries and as part of the European Renaissance. These new currents of thought have between them produced a proliferation of articles, books and new editions of Shakespeare. Less eyecatching, but no less important, are the advances in textual criticism made by scholars examining the different technical processes behind the texts of the different editions of Shakespeare, culminating in the publication of the New Oxford Shakespeare, edited by Stanley Wells and Gary Taylor (*A Textual Companion*, 1987, and *The Complete Works*, 1986). Though opinion on the investigations of these two specialists is divided, the immensity of the task accomplished makes the edition an essential tool of reference.

In *Shakespeare, Les Feux de l'Envie* ('Shakespeare, The Fires of Desire') published in 1990, René Girard discusses a number of Shakespeare's plays in terms of the theory elaborated in his earlier works, the principle of mimetic desire and the rites of violence in primitive societies. Girard's book has not been unanimously well-received by university critics – evidence of the extent to which, as James Joyce suggested in *Ulysses*, Shakespeare is being used as an ideological pawn.

More recent British and American criticism has tended to become increasingly specialized and increasingly written in a technical language not easily accessible to the layman. The most radical theorists have abandoned the quest for 'truth' altogether, and believe that 'meaning' fluctuates with time and culture and that Shakespeare's plays today are necessarily part of today's ideological strategies. Terence Hawkes, for instance, in *Meaning by Shakespeare*, claims that we 'use' *Hamlet*, rather as Hamlet 'used' *The Murder of Gonzago*, to prove something to ourselves in our world. 'Perhaps,' he says, 'its probing of the relation between art and social life, role-playing on stage and role-playing in society, appears so powerfully to offer an adequate account of important aspects of our own experience that it ends by constructing them. In other words, *Hamlet* crucially helps to determine how we perceive and respond to the world in which we live.'

François Laroque

Shakespeare multiplied: the changing perspective of criticism

Every generation recreates Shakespeare in its own image. What one age sees as his supreme merit, another ignores, to look for something quite different. It is a measure of the extraordinary complexity of Shakespeare's genius that, uniquely among great artists, he can survive this treatment.

The classical Shakespeare

During the later 17th and for most of the 18th century, criticism of Shakespeare tended to focus on his universality – his understanding of every type of human being and ability to express every kind of emotion. For these writers, Shakespeare was an untaught child of nature who seemed to have produced masterpieces almost without knowing it.

John Dryden
Dryden was the first English literary critic. Only fifty years after Shakespeare's death, his comments seem impressively balanced and objective.

To begin then with Shakespeare; he was the man who of all Modern, and perhaps Ancient Poets, had the largest and most comprehensive soul. All the Images of Nature were still present to him, and he drew them not laboriously, but luckily: when he describes any thing, you more than see it, you feel it too. Those who accuse him to have wanted learning, give him the greater commendation: he was naturally learn'd; he needed not the spectacles of Books to read Nature; he look'd inwards, and found her there. I cannot say he is every where alike; were he so, I should do him injury to compare him with the greatest of Mankind. He is many times flat, insipid; his Comick wit degenerating into clenches [puns], his serious swelling into Bombast. But he is always great, when some great occasion is presented to him: no man can say he ever had a fit subject for his wit, and did not then raise himself as high above the rest of Poets.

Of Dramatic Poesie, 1668

Nicholas Rowe

Rowe was Shakespeare's first editor and biographer.

His Plays are properly to be distinguish'd only into Comedies and Tragedies. Those which are called Histories, and even some of his Comedies, are really Tragedies, with a run or mixture of Comedy amongst 'em. That way of Trage-Comedy was the common Mistake of that Age, and is indeed become so agreeable to the English Tast, that tho' the severer Critiques among us cannot bear it, yet the generality of our Audiences seem to be better pleas'd with it than with an exact Tragedy. *The Merry Wives of Windsor, The Comedy of Errors,* and *The Taming of the Shrew,* are all pure Comedy; the rest, however they are call'd, have something of both Kinds. 'Tis not very easie to determine which way of Writing he was most Excellent in. There is certainly a great deal of Entertainment in his Comical Humours; and tho' they did not then strike at all Ranks of People, as the Satyr of the present Age has taken the Liberty to do, yet there is a pleasing and a well-distinguish'd Variety in those Characters which he thought fit to meddle with. Falstaff is allow'd by every body to be a Master-piece; the Character is always well-sustain'd, tho' drawn out into the length of three Plays; and even the Account of his Death, given by his Old Landlady Mrs.

Portia's Garden from *The Merchant of Venice,* an engraving of 1795 after William Hodges. Its classical design is inspired by Poussin or Claude.

Quickly, in the first Act of *Henry V*, tho' it be extremely Natural, is yet as diverting as any Part of his Life.

Some Account of the Life of Mr. William Shakespeare, 1709

Alexander Pope

His Characters are so much Nature her self, that 'tis a sort of injury to call them by so distant a name as Copies of her. Those of other Poets have a constant resemblance, which shews that they receiv'd them from one another, and were but multiplyers of the same image: each picture like a mock-rainbow is but the reflection of a reflection. But every single character in Shakespear is as much an Individual, as those in Life itself; it is as impossible to find any two alike; and such as from their relation or affinity in any respect appear most to be Twins, will upon comparison be

D*avid Garrick as Richard III*, an engraving after William Hogarth, *c*. 1745, showing the king awakening from his nightmare before the battle.

found remarkably distinct. To this life and variety of Character, we must add the wonderful Preservation of it; which is such throughout his plays, that had all the Speeches been printed without the very names of the Persons, I believe one might have apply'd them with certainty to every speaker.

The Preface to Shakespeare's Works, 1725

Samuel Johnson

Johnson summed up the Augustan view of Shakespeare. Largely unresponsive to his poetry, he valued him (unlike Pope) for his ability to generalize human nature and to dramatize moral choices.

Nothing can please many, and please long, but just representations of general nature. Particular manners can be known to few, and therefore few only can judge how nearly they are copied. The irregular combinations of fanciful invention may delight a-while, by that novelty of which the common satiety of life sends us all in quest; but the pleasures of sudden wonder are soon exhausted, and the mind can only repose on the stability of truth.

Shakespeare is above all writers, at least above all modern writers, the poet of nature; the poet that holds up to his readers a faithful mirror of manners and of life. His characters are not modified by the customs of particular places, unpractised by the rest of the world; by the peculiarities of studies or professions, which can operate but upon small numbers; or by the accidents of transient fashions or temporary opinions: they are the genuine progeny of common humanity, such as the world will always supply, and observation will always find. His persons act and speak by the influence

of those general passions and principles by which all minds are agitated, and the whole system of life is continued in motion. In the writings of other poets a character is too often an individual; in those of Shakespeare it is commonly a species.

Preface to Shakespeare, 1765

The Romantic Shakespeare

The generation of Wordsworth, Coleridge and Lamb drastically reversed the Augustan judgment. Shakespeare's indifference to the classical rules, his spontaneous expression of extreme emotion, above all his language, became for them the essence of his genius. Significantly, he is now seen as a poet to be read, not a playwright to be experienced in the theatre.

Charles Lamb

It may seem a paradox, but I cannot help being of opinion that the plays of Shakspeare are less calculated for performance on a stage, than those of almost any other dramatist whatever. Their distinguishing excellence is a reason that they should be so. There is so much in them, which comes not under the province of acting, with which eye, and tone, and gesture, have nothing to do.... The sublime images, the poetry alone, is that which is present to our minds in the reading.

So to see Lear acted, – to see an old man tottering about the stage with a walking-stick, turned out of doors by his daughters in a rainy night, has nothing in it but what is painful and disgusting. We want to take him into shelter and relieve him. That is all the feeling which the acting of Lear ever produced in me. But the Lear of

Shakspeare cannot be acted. The contemptible machinery by which they mimic the storm which he goes out in, is not more inadequate to represent the horrors of the real elements, than any actor can be to represent Lear: they might more easily propose to personate the Satan of Milton upon a stage, or one of Michael Angelo's terrible figures. The greatness of Lear is not in corporal dimension, but in intellectual: the explosions of his passion are terrible as a volcano: they are storms turning up and disclosing to the bottom that sea, his mind, with all its vast riches. It is his mind which is laid bare.

On the Tragedies of Shakespeare, 1811

Samuel Taylor Coleridge

Coleridge's Shakespeare is even more withdrawn from the common man than Lamb's. He is a philosopher, a sublime and exalted thinker, whose very obscurity is a mark of his genius.

It has been before observed that images, however beautiful, though faithfully copied from nature, and as accurately represented in words, do not of themselves characterize the poet. They become proofs of original genius only as far as they are modified by a predominant passion; or by associated thoughts or images awakened by that passion; or when they have the effect of reducing multitude to unity, or succession to an instant; or lastly, when a human and intellectual life is transferred to them from the poet's own spirit.

Biographia Literaria, 1817

Shakspeare possessed the chief, if not every, requisite of a poet, – deep feeling and exquisite sense of beauty, both as exhibited to the eye in the combinations of form, and to the ear in sweet and appropriate melody; that these feelings were under the command of his own will; that in his very first productions he projected his mind out of his own particular being, and felt, and made others feel, on subjects no way connected with himself, except by force of contemplation and that

Keats had a bust of Shakespeare on his inkwell.

sublime faculty by which a great mind becomes that, on which it meditates.
Lectures, 1818

Shakspeare is of no age. It is idle to endeavour to support his phrases by quotations from Ben Jonson, Beaumont and Fletcher, &c. His language is entirely his own, and the younger dramatists imitated him. The construction of Shakspeare's sentences, whether in verse or prose, is the necessary and homogeneous vehicle of his peculiar manner of thinking. His is not the style of the age....

I believe Shakspeare was not a whit more intelligible in his own day than he is now to an educated man, except for a few local allusions of no consequence. As I said, he is of no age – nor, I may add, of any religion, or party, or profession. The body and substance of his works came out of the unfathomable depths of his own oceanic mind: his observation and reading, which was considerable, supplied him with the drapery of his figures.
Table Talk, 1836

John Keats
Keats' comments on Shakespeare consist of remarks in letters or the margins of his copy of the plays, and he made no attempt to develop them. Yet they are among the most perceptive made by any critic, and are especially valuable coming from a poet of such genius. He was especially struck by Shakespeare's apparent ability to lose his own identity in that of other beings, an ability which for him lay at the root of poetry.

Several things dovetailed in my mind, & at once it struck me, what quality went to form a Man of Achievement, especially in Literature, & which Shakespeare possessed so enormously – I mean *Negative Capability*, that is when a man is capable of being in uncertainties, Mysteries, doubts, without any irritable reaching after fact & reason.
Letter of 21 December 1817

The excellence of every art is its intensity, capable of making all disagreeables evaporate from their being in close relationship with Beauty and Truth. Examine 'King Lear', and you will find this exemplified throughout.
Letter of 28 December 1817

WRITTEN BEFORE RE-READING KING LEAR
O golden-tongued Romance with serene lute!
Fair plumed Syren! Queen of far away!
Leave melodizing on this wintry day,
Shut up thine olden volume, and be mute.
Adieu! for once again the fierce dispute,
Betwixt damnation and impassioned clay
Must I burn through; once more assay
The bitter-sweet of this Shakespearean fruit.
Chief Poet! and ye clouds of Albion,
Begetters of our deep eternal theme,
When through the old oak forest I am gone
Let me not wander in a barren dream,
But when I am consumed with the Fire,
Give me new Phoenix-wings to fly at my desire.
22 January 1818

William Hazlitt

It was Hazlitt who began seriously to explore the psychological aspect of Shakespeare's plays, an approach that dominated criticism throughout the 19th century and up to our own time. The technique of 'character analysis' was born.

Each of his characters is as much itself, and as absolutely independent of the rest, as well as of the author, as if they were living persons, not fictions of the mind. The poet may be said, for the time, to identify himself with the character he wishes to represent, and to pass from one to another, like the same soul successively animating different bodies. By an art like that of the ventriloquist, he throws his imagination out of himself, and makes every word appear to proceed from the mouth of the person in whose name it is given. His plays alone are properly expressions of the passions, not descriptions of them. His characters are real beings of flesh and blood; they speak like men, not like authors. One might suppose that he had stood by at the time and overheard what passed. As in our dreams we hold conversations with ourselves, make remarks, or communicate intelligence, and have no idea of the answer which we shall receive, and which we ourselves make, till we hear it: so the dialogues in

King Hamlet's ghost, seen through Romantic eyes, a late 18th-century engraving after a painting by Henry Fuseli.

Shakespeare are carried on without any consciousness of what is to follow, without any appearance of preparation or premeditation. The gusts of passion come and go like sounds of music borne on the wind. Nothing is made out by formal inference and analogy, by climax and antithesis: all comes, or seems to come, immediately from nature. Each object and circumstance exists in his mind, as it would have existed in reality: each several train of thought and feeling goes on of itself, without confusion or effort. In the world of his imagination, everything has a life, a place and being of its own!

Lectures on the English Poets, 1818

A.C. Bradley

Bradley was the supreme practitioner of character analysis, and his detailed comments on individual Shakespearean characters are still valuable. But when he attempted to define the nature of Shakespearean tragedy he propounded a theory of the hero's 'tragic flaw', which, while archetypically Romantic, may now seem as remote from our time as it does from Shakespeare's.

His tragic characters are made of the stuff we find within ourselves and within the persons who surround them. But, by an intensification of the life which they share with others, they are raised above them; and the greatest are raised so far that, if we fully realise all that is implied in their words and actions, we become conscious that in real life we have known scarcely any one resembling them. Some, like Hamlet and Cleopatra, have genius. Others, like Othello, Lear, Macbeth, Coriolanus, are built on the grand scale; and desire, passion, or will attains

in them a terrible force. In almost all we observe a marked one-sidedness, a predisposition in some particular direction; a total incapacity, in certain circumstances, of resisting the force which draws in this direction; a fatal tendency to identify the whole being with one interest, object, passion, or habit of mind. This, it would seem, is, for Shakespeare, the fundamental tragic trait.... It is a fatal gift, but it carries with it a touch of greatness; and when there is joined to it nobility of mind, or genius, or immense force, we realise the full power and reach of the soul, and the conflict in which it engages acquires that magnitude which stirs not only sympathy and pity, but admiration, terror, and awe....

In the circumstances where we see the hero placed, his tragic trait, which is also his greatness, is fatal to him. To meet these circumstances something is required which a smaller man might have given, but which the hero cannot give. He errs, by action or omission; and his error, joining with other causes, brings on him ruin.

Hence, in the first place, a Shakespearean tragedy is never, like some miscalled tragedies, depressing. No one ever closes the book with the feeling that man is a poor mean creature. He may be wretched and he may be awful, but he is not small. His lot may be heart-rending and mysterious, but it is not contemptible. The most confirmed of cynics ceases to be a cynic while he reads these plays. And with this greatness of the tragic hero (which is not always confined to him) is connected, secondly, what I venture to describe as the centre of the tragic impression. This central feeling is the impression of waste.

With Shakespeare, at any rate, the pity and fear which are stirred by the tragic story seem to unite with, and even to merge in, a profound sense of sadness and mystery, which is due to this impression of waste. 'What a piece of work is man,' we cry; 'so much more beautiful and so much more terrible than we knew! Why should he be so if this beauty and greatness only tortures itself and throws itself away?' We seem to have before us a type of the mystery of the whole world, the tragic fact which extends far beyond the limits of tragedy.

Shakespearean Tragedy, 1904

Dissenting views

There have always been those who thought Shakespeare overrated. Ironically, these critics include two of the greatest minds in European literature.

Voltaire

For Voltaire, Shakespeare was a barbarian. He did not deny his talent, but was revolted by his lack of classical decorum.

Shakespeare boasted a strong, fruitful genius. He was natural and sublime, but had not so much as a single spark of good taste, or knew one rule of the drama.

Lettres philosophiques, 1733

Everywhere, the common people are pleased by astonishing events; they love to see scene-changes, coronations of kings, processions, fights, murders, witches, ceremonies, weddings, burials; they rush to these things in crowds and carry along with them others who are ready to forgive their enormous faults if there are also a few beauties, and even if there are not.

Letter to the Académie
Française, 1776

[On *Hamlet*] This vulgar and barbarous play would not be supported by the lowest public of France or Italy. In it Hamlet goes mad in the second act, and his mistress in the third; the prince kills his mistress's father, pretending to kill a rat, and the heroine throws herself into the river. Her grave is dug on the stage; the grave-diggers utter doubtful pleasantries worthy of them, whilst holding skulls in their hands; prince Hamlet replies to their abominable vulgarities with no less disgusting idiocies. Meanwhile, one of the characters conquers Poland. Hamlet, his mother and his stepfather drink together on the stage; they sing at table, quarrel, fight, and kill each other. One would take this work to be the fruit of the inspiration of a drunken savage.

*Appel à toutes les nations
de l'Europe*, 1761

Leo Tolstoy

Tolstoy's objection to Shakespeare was partly that his language was unnatural, but mainly that he had no significant moral message.

I remember the astonishment I felt when I first read Shakespeare. I expected to receive a powerful aesthetic pleasure, but having read, one after the other, works regarded as his best, *King Lear*, *Romeo and Juliet*, *Hamlet*, and *Macbeth*, not only did I feel no delight, but I felt an irresistible repulsion and tedium, and doubted as to whether I was senseless in feeling works regarded as the summit of perfection by the whole of the civilized world to be trivial and positively bad, or whether the significance which this civilized world attributes to the works of Shakespeare was itself senseless. My consternation was increased by the fact that I always keenly felt the beauties of poetry in every form; then why should artistic works recognized by the whole world as those of a genius – the works of Shakespeare – not only fail to please me, but be disagreeable to me?...

All his characters speak, not their own, but always one and the same Shakespearean pretentious and unnatural language, in which not only they could not speak, but in which no living man ever has spoken or does speak.... From his first words, exaggeration is seen: the exaggeration of events, the exaggeration of emotion, and the exaggeration of effects. One sees at once that he does not believe in what he says, that it is of no necessity to him, that he invents the events he describes and is indifferent to his characters – that he has conceived them only for the stage and therefore makes them do and say only what may strike his public, and so we do not believe either in the events or in the actions or in the sufferings of the characters.

He alone can write a drama who has got something to say to men, and that something of the greatest importance for them: about man's relation to God, to the Universe, to the All, the Eternal, the Infinite. But when, thanks to the German theories about objective art, the idea was established that for the drama this was quite unnecessary, then it became obvious how a writer like Shakespeare – who had not got developed in his mind the religious convictions proper to his time, who, in fact, had no convictions at all, but heaped up in his drama all possible events, horrors, fooleries, discussions, and effects – could appear to be a dramatic writer of the greatest genius.

But these are all external reasons. The fundamental inner cause of Shakespeare's fame was and is this – that his dramas ... corresponded to the irreligious and immoral frame of mind of the upper classes of his time and ours.

Shakespeare and the Drama, 1906

George Bernard Shaw

Like Tolstoy, Shaw was irritated by the uncritical adulation given to Shakespeare, whom he considered (in comparison with such writers as Henrik Ibsen and himself) to be lacking in ideas and depressingly bourgeois in his attitude to social questions.

A *Study for King Lear*, painted *c.* 1773 by Sir Joshua Reynolds.

Once or twice we scent an anticipation of the crudest side of Ibsen's polemics on the Woman Question, as in *All's Well that Ends Well*, where the man cuts as meanly selfish a figure beside his enlightened lady doctor wife as Helmer beside Nora; or in *Cymbeline*, where Posthumus, having, as he believes, killed his wife for inconstancy, speculates for a moment on what his life would have been worth if the same standard of continence had been applied to himself. And certainly no modern study of the voluptuous temperament, and the spurious heroism and heroinism which its ecstasies produce, can add much to *Antony and Cleopatra*, unless it were some sense of the spuriousness on the author's part. But search for statesmanship, or even citizenship, or any sense of the commonwealth, material or spiritual, and you will not find the making of a decent vestryman or curate in the whole horde. As to faith, hope, courage, conviction, or any of the true heroic qualities, you find nothing but death made sensational, despair made stage-sublime, sex made romantic, and barrenness covered up by sentimentality and the mechanical lilt of blank verse.

All that you miss in Shakespear you find in Bunyan, to whom the true heroic came quite obviously and naturally. The world was to him a more terrible place than it was to Shakespear; but he saw through it a path at the end of which a man might look not only forward to the Celestial City, but back on his life and say:– 'Tho' with great difficulty I am got hither, yet now I do not repent me of all the trouble I have been at to arrive where I am. My sword I give to him that shall succeed me in my pilgrimage, and my courage and

skill to him that can get them.' The heart vibrates like a bell to such an utterance as this: to turn from it to 'Out, out, brief candle,' and 'The rest is silence,' and 'We are such stuff as dreams are made of; and our little life is rounded by a sleep' is to turn from life, strength, resolution, morning air and eternal youth, to the terrors of a drunken nightmare.

Saturday Review, January 1896

And then Touchstone, with his rare jests about the knight that swore by his honor they were good pancakes! Who would endure such humor from anyone but Shakespear? – an Eskimo would demand his money back if a modern author offered him such fare. And the comfortable old Duke, symbolical of the British villa dweller, who likes to find 'sermons in stones and good in everything,' and then to have a good dinner! This unvenerable impostor, expanding on his mixed diet of pious twaddle and venison, rouses my worst passions. Even when Shakespear, in his efforts to be a social philosopher, does rise for an instant to the level of a sixth-rate Kingsley, his solemn self-complacency infuriates me. And yet, so wonderful is his art, that it is not easy to disentangle what is unbearable from what is irresistible. Orlando one moment says:

> Whate'er you are
> That in this desert inaccessible
> Under the shade of melancholy
>   boughs
> Lose and neglect the creeping hours
>   of time,

which, though it indicates a thoroughly unhealthy imagination, and would have been impossible to, for instance,

Chaucer, is yet magically fine of its kind. The next moment he tacks on lines which would have revolted Mr Pecksniff:

> If ever you have looked on better days,
> If ever been where bells have knolled to church,
>> [*How perfectly the atmosphere of the rented pew is caught in this incredible line!*]
> If ever sat at any good man's feast,
> If ever from your eyelids wiped–

I really shall get sick if I quote any more of it. Was ever such canting, snivelling, hypocritical unctuousness exuded by an actor anxious to shew that he was above his profession, and was a thoroughly respectable man in private life?
Saturday Review, December 1896

Gary Taylor

In modern times, Shakespeare has come under fire from those who, for all their admiration, prefer to stay (in Ben Jonson's words) 'this side idolatry', and feel bound to point out that he had his limitations. For the Shakespearean scholar and editor Gary Taylor, as for Tolstoy and Shaw, these limitations are very largely moral ones.

To take just one example, *Measure for Measure* tells the story of a puritanical governor who sets out to eliminate sexual corruption in Vienna. Shakespeare tells the story in a way that repeatedly undercuts this ambition. Angelo, the governor, himself succumbs to lust; the most visible victims of his crusade are a likable young engaged couple, guilty of nothing more heinous than consummation before consecration (dessert before saying grace). By concentrating upon the hypocritical governor and the unlucky lovers, Shakespeare distracts attention from the real focus of sexual corruption, Viennese prostitution. The sex industry is represented in his play by a ... crew of harmless comics: dumb

John Everett Millais' famous painting of the death of Ophelia (1851–2) is a literal rendering of the Queen's description in *Hamlet*.

customer, daffy pimp, dizzy madam.
The names themselves assure us that
we have entered the world of happy
whoredom. But where, pray tell, are
the prostitutes?

Shakespeare shows us the customers
and the management, but the sexual
work force itself, the women who ride
up and down the shaft to the coal
mines of prostitution, them we never
see, never hear, hardly hear of. The
worst punishment that can be devised
for Lucio, at the play's end, a
punishment many modern critics
consider neurotically severe (on the
Duke's part or Shakespeare's), is
'Marrying a punk' – being forced to
husband a prostitute he had
impregnated. Likewise, in *Pericles* we
see the husband-and-wife duo of
brothel owners comically complaining
about the local whore shortage, and we
see their eager underling Bolt (a name
both phallic and functional, since he
bolts the door); but nary a prostitute
do we see. The management buys and
then tries to sell Marina; but she, in a
delectable little dramatic fantasy,
moralizes the lust out of her customers,
so that they pay her for sermons
instead of sex. Indeed, one of them,
who happens happily to be the most
eligible bachelor in town, falls in love
with her and, in due course, proposes
marriage.

Shakespeare wasted no sympathy on
the women lured or conned or forced
into prostitution. The working women
who do appear in his plays are accused
of murdering their customers outright
(Doll Tearsheet, in *Henry IV, Part 2*)
or of murdering them piecemeal, with
disease (Phrynia and Timandra, in
Timon of Athens), in both cases
without compunction or compulsion.

Shakespeare's contemporary Thomas
Middleton could sympathize with the
'Distressed needlewomen and trade-
fallne wives', the 'poore spirits' and
'poore shifting sisters', 'hungry things'
caught on the 'hooke' baited by urban
pimps; but Shakespeare himself never
considers, or asks his audience to
consider, the circumstances or motives
of such women.

Shakespeare sees prostitution from
the outside, or rather from the male
side, the side of the customer or the
pimp; the women either do not exist
at all (as in *Measure for Measure* and
Pericles) or deserve contempt (as in
Henry IV, Part 2 and *Timon of Athens*).
Curiously, unrealistically, they are
never young, never beautiful, never
genuinely alluring. To make them
attractive would be to admit their
power.

Reinventing Shakespeare, 1990

The modern Shakespeare

*As the Shakespeare industry has gathered
momentum in the 20th century, the
number of perspectives on his work
has multiplied. He has been interpreted
by Freudians, Marxists, anthropologists,
linguists, feminists, philosophers, and
literary theorists of every persuasion.*

Political relevance
*Jan Kott fought against the Nazis in the
Polish underground movement, and
then suffered under Stalinism.
His Shakespeare is a realist, not a
Romantic.*

Every historical period finds in him
what it is looking for and what it wants
to see. A reader or spectator in the
mid-twentieth century interprets

Richard III through his own experiences. He cannot do otherwise. And that is why he is not terrified – or rather, not amazed – at Shakespeare's cruelty. He views the struggle for power and the mutual slaughter of the characters far more calmly than did many generations of spectators and critics in the nineteenth century. More calmly, or, at any rate, more rationally. Cruel death, suffered by most *dramatis personae*, is not regarded today as an aesthetic necessity, or as an essential rule in tragedy in order to produce *catharsis*, or even as a specific characteristic of Shakespeare's genius. The violent deaths of the principal characters are now regarded rather as an historical necessity, or as something altogether natural. Even in *Titus Andronicus*, written, or rewritten, by Shakespeare probably in the same year as *King Richard III*, modern audiences see much more than the ludicrous and grotesque accumulation of needless horrors which nineteenth century critics found in it. And when *Titus Andronicus* received a production like that by Peter Brook, today's audiences were ready to applaud the general slaughter in act five no less enthusiastically than Elizabethan coppersmiths, taylors, butchers and soldiers had done. In those days the play was one of the greatest theatrical successes. By discovering in Shakespeare's plays problems that are relevant to our own time, modern audiences often, unexpectedly, find themselves near to the Elizabethans; or at least are in the position to understand them well. This is particularly true of the Histories.

Shakespeare Our Contemporary, 1964

Theatrical convention

It is no longer customary to stress the 'naturalness' of Shakespeare's plays, and to treat the characters as if they were real people. Plays are artificial constructs, with determining conventions of their own.

We must remember that our illusion in the theatre is entirely different from that of the Elizabethans.... Our drama is enacted under the tacit agreement that there are no spectators present. Only one wall, that in front of the audience, is wanting to the scene. In contrast to this, Shakespeare's stage is surrounded by the spectators on three sides. The actor may be said to stand in the midst of the audience; he is always mindful of this while he is acting, and evidently in many cases directly addresses his spectators.... This relation is evidenced by the monologue, in which the speaker, so to say, fraternizes with the audience, and the whole dramatic composition and the illusion connected with it may in this manner be absolutely destroyed. It is no longer a monologue in the proper sense – i.e. the expression of an individual who, thinking aloud, renders account of his most intimate thoughts and feelings – but a means which the author uses in order to instruct his audience about the events, or about the plans and character of the personage speaking. Such instruction and explanation is further emphasized by the form in which the actor delivering the monologue addresses the audience; e.g. 'And mark how well the sequel hangs together', or 'To say the truth', or 'Mark me now'.... This use of elements which according to our present view contradict the essence of the monologue forms a peculiar feature of Shakespeare's monologues in every period of his art, and most clearly appears in the latest products of his riper years.

L.L. Schücking
Character Problems in Shakespeare's Plays, 1922

A feminist Shakespeare

The rise of feminist criticism has been one of the most fruitful developments of the last few decades. Some classic authors have been found wanting. Shakespeare, however, seems to pass this test too.

Patriarchal order takes different forms... throughout the Shakespearean canon. In some comedies it weighs lightly: the power of the father or ruler can be evaded in a green world retreat or countered by the activities of the heroines. Yet at the conclusions of the comedies, the assertiveness of Kate, Rosalind, and others is muted as they declare or imply their submission to their husbands. Elsewhere patriarchy is more oppressive. Its lethal flaws are made manifest in the presentation of rape and attempted rape, in the aggressive, death-dealing feud of *Romeo and Juliet*, in the spurious manliness and empty honor that generate the tragedy of *Othello*, in the militaristic and mercantile values of the Greeks in *Troilus and Cressida* and of the Romans in *Antony and Cleopatra*. Many other plays as well reveal the high cost of patriarchal values; the men who uphold them atrophy, and the women, whether resistant or acquiescent, die. Although women may strive to resist or to correct the perversions of patriarchy, they do not succeed in altering that order, nor do they withdraw their allegiance from

it. Cordelia... stands up to her father's coercion out of love for him and leads an army on behalf of his 'right;' she dies a victim of a chain of brutal assertions of manhood... In *King Lear* and elsewhere the extent to which Shakespeare aligns himself with patriarchy, merely portrays it or deliberately criticizes it remains a complex and open question, one that feminist criticism is aptly suited to address.

Carolyn Ruth Swift Lenz, Gayle Greene and Carol Thomas Neely
The Woman's Part, 1980

The female who is chaste and constant is symbolically a guarantee of moral virtue in men who remain linked with her. Whether he is father, husband, lover, or brother, a man who honors his bond to a chaste constant heroine symbolically honors 'feminine' ends, and thus is devoted to the right use of power. In *Love's Labour's Lost*, constancy is opposed to fickleness which arises from ignorance of one's own emotions and to egotism. It thus becomes a shorthand way of suggesting an ultimate reality, an unswerving set of values and the faith necessary to maintain fidelity to insubstantial and powerless ends. In *A Midsummer Night's Dream*, constancy is a cosmic virtue, a larger purpose containing all human purposes, and triumphant over folly and delusion. Chaste constancy swiftly becomes the cornerstone, the pivot, the crucial element in Shakespeare's morality. It has this semi-divine nature only in women because it symbolizes 'feminine' qualities of harmony, community, tolerance, moral flexibility (within limits), pity, compassion, forgiveness, and loving nutritiveness. These qualities are seen as the ultimate

The American artist Sandra Fisher painted Bob Wisdom, a black American actor, as Othello in *From 'Othello'*, 1991.

moral goods, the things all humans really need and want, or would if they were not blind. In Shakespeare's division of experience, however, men cannot be forced to revere these things. The process of coming to recognize these goods is a process of education in seeing.

Chaste constancy has several functions in the comedies from *Two Gentlemen* to *Twelfth Night* and *Much Ado*. It offers a reliable and immovable moral good that is visible in the world; thus it contrasts with male legitimacy, a set of men and institutions which claim to stand for moral good but which are untrustworthy and delusive. Second, it confers on females an equality of a sort with males. Males possess freedom and power-in-the-world; chaste constant women are bound to inlaw [naturally benevolent] feminine ends and modes, but they possess moral superiority over men. This superiority is never offensive to male supremacists, however, because chaste constant heroines are utterly devoted to the male world, and usually to one man. That man is the center of her being, the only and wholly significant object of her desire. Because the man is so important to her, her entire existence is bent towards him. Her moral superiority is therefore not so much a power over him as it is an excellence, like her beauty or wit or wisdom, placed at his service.

Marilyn French
Shakespeare's Division of Experience,
1982

Productions and interpretations of Shakespeare's plays

Following the historical reconstructions of the Victorians, the early 20th century brought a return to the simplicity of Elizabethan stage sets. Modern productions have played a large part in the continuing success of Shakespeare's plays.

The Elizabethan stage of Shakespeare's day was fairly rudimentary, and the stage sets of a symbolic or merely indicative character. Painted scenes in the Italian style barely featured, other than in the baroque sets of the masques performed at Court. In the absence of visual realism, an effort was made to create spectacular effects with fight scenes, mime, simulated thunder, the use of fire-crackers, and bags of bull's blood to suggest bloodshed on stage. But it was above all the text and actor's voice that generated the action and impressed it on the audience's imagination; thus Hamlet advised the actors who had come to Elsinore to speak their speeches 'trippingly on the tongue' (*Hamlet*, Act III.ii.).

The plays were performed in the county towns of England and sometimes at sea, on board ship, as well as in London; there were also foreign tours: for example, English actors put on *The Merchant of Venice* in Germany in 1611.

After the theatres were destroyed after the Civil War by order of Parliament (1642), the Restoration (1660) found inspiration in the stage techniques current in France, adopting the proscenium arch, which made visual illusion possible. The other great innovation was that female roles were from this time onwards played by actresses. At this period Shakespeare's plays were adapted to suit contemporary taste by dramatists such as Sir William Davenant, John Dryden and Nahum Tate.

In the 18th century the English stage was dominated by the actor David Garrick (1717–79), who was also manager of the Drury Lane Theatre in London from 1747 to 1776. He

Mr Garrick as King Lear.

worked hard to make Shakespeare into a national institution, even if his adaptations sometimes departed considerably from the original. The period was, indeed, marked by the rise of great actors, the first 'stars' of the stage, who owed their success to the Shakespearean repertoire. The Irish actor Charles Macklin (1699–1797) distinguished himself in his rendering, in 1741, of the part of Shylock, the Jew in *The Merchant of Venice*, a part he played again in 1789 when he was ninety years old. Charles Kemble (1775–1854) played many Shakespearean parts, but the most memorable was that of King John, which he performed at Covent Garden in 1823, launching the fashion for period dress and elaborate historical reconstructions. His brother John Philip (1757–1823) managed the theatres of Drury Lane and Covent Garden, while also distinguishing himself as an actor and producer of the great tragedies and the Roman plays. But the greatest of all was undoubtedly Edmund Kean (1787–1833), whose first successes were in Drury Lane, in the role of Shylock in 1814 and then of Richard III; he also played the leading parts in the great tragedies: *Hamlet, Othello, King Lear, Macbeth.*

The actor William Macready (1793–1873), who managed the Covent Garden Theatre and then the Drury Lane Theatre, played most of the great tragic roles. His chief merit was that he abandoned the adaptations that were then still the rule in favour of Shakespeare's original texts.

The Victorian age was marked principally by the taste for historical reconstruction and visual display in theatrical productions – a fashion

John Philip Kemble as Hamlet, 1783.

initiated by Sir Henry Irving (1838–1905), manager of the Lyceum Theatre from 1878 to 1902, and Sir Herbert Beerbohm Tree (1853–1917), manager of the Haymarket Theatre from 1887 to 1897.

In reaction to this emphasis on the spectacular, which tended to make performances distinctly heavy, William Poel (1852–1934) sought to recreate the conditions under which the Elizabethan stage had operated. He put on a shortened version of *Hamlet*, taken from the first quarto, without scenery or interval. He had a profound influence on actors such as Harley Granville-Barker (1877–1946), who became famous for his productions of comedies, for example *The Winter's Tale, Twelfth Night* and *A Midsummer Night's Dream*, which he staged between 1912 and 1914. This marked the beginning of a great theatrical revival which spread rapidly throughout Europe.

The 20th century was responsible for a number of innovations. For example, Sir Barry Jackson (1879–1961) in 1925 staged *Hamlet* in modern dress, one way of asserting the reality of Shakespeare in contemporary life. Sir Tyrone Guthrie (1900–1971) successfully repeated this experiment in his 1953 production of *All's Well That Ends Well*, a play relatively rarely performed until then, which he helped to rediscover. Such modernism made it possible to transpose the plays into a new context – an idea that underlay the success, hailed as one of the most remarkable in the theatre, of *A Midsummer Night's Dream* staged by Peter Brook (born 1925) at Stratford in 1970. In this production he used the world of the

Sir Johnston Forbes-Robertson as Hamlet, 1902.

circus as the modern equivalent of the magic and fairyland of the Athenian forest in which the young lovers take refuge. The cosmopolitan, multi-racial and multi-cultural character of Peter Brook's company added to the originality of his productions. The accents and intonations of actors of British, African, Japanese and Indian origin give a different and often unexpected resonance to Shakespeare's lines. In an altogether different spirit, French director Ariane Mnouchkine found inspiration in the traditions of Japanese theatre (*kabuki* and *noh*) in her 1981 production of *Richard II* at the Théâtre du Soleil in Vincennes. This play marked an epoch and influenced many productions in England and elsewhere.

In the mid-1970s the British producer Terry Hands, member of the Royal Shakespeare Company, went to work at the Comédie Française in Paris to stage a number of Shakespeare's plays, notably *The Merchant of Venice* and a memorable *Twelfth Night* (1976). In Italy the productions of Giorgio Strehler at the Piccolo Teatro in Milan (*King Lear, The Tempest*) are also recognized as brilliant and a model of their kind.

The 1980s allowed a wider public to become acquainted with the world of Shakespeare, thanks to the British Broadcasting Corporation's production of the complete canon, thirty-six plays in all.

The great actors

They are too numerous for all to be named. But the most outstanding remains without a doubt John Gielgud in the part of Hamlet.

In England the Shakespearean repertoire remains an obligatory rite of passage in the career of every great actor or actress. Only to consider *Hamlet*, the best known and arguably the greatest of Shakespeare's plays, the list of the great renderings of the part of the melancholy prince of Denmark is long indeed.... In the romantic period the great actors were John Philip Kemble, Edmund Kean and William Macready, whom Sir Henry Irving succeeded at the Lyceum in 1874, when the fashion was for lavish productions. Sir Johnston Forbes-Robertson (1853–1937) played the title role in an 1897 production, and went on to act it in a silent movie of 1913. Hamlet was also played by a woman, Sarah Bernhardt, in 1899. Sir Frank Robert Benson (1858–1939) was the first to put on the play in its complete original text at the Lyceum in 1899. In the United States in 1922 John Barrymore played the part more than a hundred times to spellbound audiences. Barry Jackson's Hamlet in modern dress in 1925 was a landmark, though the rendering by John Gielgud at the Old Vic in London in 1930, in which Hamlet was portrayed as the representative of a disillusioned generation, is still regarded by many critics as the best of the century. It was in 1937, in Tyrone Guthrie's production, that Laurence Olivier (1907–1991) played the part, to which he returned on screen ten years later. Alec Guinness also did a memorable rendering in a production at the Old Vic in 1938.

After the war the part was interpreted by Paul Scofield in 1948, Michael Redgrave at the Old Vic in 1950, then at Stratford eight years later. Peter O'Toole played Hamlet, directed

J ohn Gielgud as Hamlet, 1934.

by Laurence Olivier, in 1963 for the opening of London's National Theatre, while another actor, who won fame on the screen but was trained by the Royal Shakespeare Company, Richard Burton, played the part in New York in 1964. Hamlet was then acted by David Warner at Stratford and in London in 1965–6, and by Alan Howard in 1970. Ben Kingsley played a neuropathic Hamlet in a production staged in modern dress at the little Stratford theatre, The Other Place, by a young woman who died prematurely, Buzz Goodbody. Then came the

Thus Matthew Locke and Pelham Humfrey staged *The Tempest* in 1674. A little later Henry Purcell wrote his semi-opera *The Fairy Queen*, a version of *A Midsummer Night's Dream* in which sung passages alternate with spoken text. In the 18th century it continued to be the comedies that found favour with adapters: in 1716 the English singer and songwriter Richard Leveridge used extracts from *A Midsummer Night's Dream*, calling them *Pyramus and Thisbe* after the burlesque play within a play performed by the artisans. In 1744 the Italian

Laurence Olivier as Henry V in 1944.

Peter Brook's epoch-making 1970 production of *A Midsummer Night's Dream* with the Royal Shakespeare Company.

interpretations of Derek Jacobi: first in 1978, again in Jonathan Pryce and Michael Pennington's film for the BBC in 1980, and yet again in Anton Lesser's film in 1982. Finally the part was tackled by a young actor, Mark Rylance, who rendered Hamlet as a complete psychotic, dressed in striped pyjamas, as if Denmark were to him a vast psychiatric hospital.

Shakespeare and the opera

Shakespeare's plays have often been adapted for operas based on specific scenes or characters, one such being Falstaff, whom Giuseppe Verdi made the subject of an opera in 1893.

In the 17th century it was the comedies that inspired musicians and librettists.

composer Francesco Maria Veracini transposed *As You Like It*, taking his title, *Rosalind*, from the main character. It is known, too, that Mozart, shortly before he died, dreamed of composing music for an opera based on *The Tempest*. Towards the end of the century adaptations of the tragedies were also produced, with Benda and Swanenberg's *Romeo and Juliet* in 1776.

In the 19th century it was Shakespeare's great tragedies that chiefly inspired the world of opera. *Romeo and Juliet* was frequently an inspiration to romantic composers, yielding two great operas, one by Vincenzo Bellini in 1830, the other by Charles Gounod in 1867. Gioacchino Rossini's *Othello,* composed in 1816, is still famous for its willow song. Verdi presented *Macbeth* in 1847 and revised it in 1865. In this opera the music evokes the inner world of the conscience (Macbeth's crime, the queen's sleepwalking), as much as the outward action of the witches, animal cries, and the choir of people suffering tyranny. In 1887, Verdi then composed his own version of *Othello* in which the essence of the conflict was reduced by Arrigo Boito's masterly adaptation to a vehicle for musical expression. But perhaps greatest of all Shakespearean operas is Verdi's *Falstaff* (1893), adapted by Boito from *The Merry Wives of Windsor*, with added touches (like the aria on 'honour') taken from the Henry IV plays. Verdi also contemplated writing an opera based on *King Lear* at the end of his life, but unfortunately the project was never started. Wagner attempted a Shakespearean theme only once; his early opera *Das Liebesverbot*, ('The Prohibition of Love', 1836), was

Poster for Verdi's *Otello*.

based on *Measure for Measure*.

The 20th century brought a return to the comedies, with Bedrich Smetana's *Viola* (1924), based on *Twelfth Night*, and *A Midsummer Night's Dream*, composed by Benjamin Britten in 1960. In the latter opera the voices are used to express the opposition of the supernatural world of the forest to the world of humans. By including familiar popular tunes, Britten successfully preserved the humorous effects of the play.

François Laroque

Shakespeare in the cinema

The history of the plays, the great productions and performances, highlights the important relationship of stage and screen. From the start of cinema to the present day, Shakespeare has inspired producers as different as Georges Méliès, Orson Welles, Akira Kurosawa and Peter Greenaway.

The age of silent cinema was not the least prolific, and one can count, in the first three decades of the 20th century, seventeen *Hamlets*, ten *Julius Caesars*, eight *Macbeths*, ten *Merchants of Venice*.... Most of these films, despite the contributions of film directors such as Georges Méliès or David Lewelyn Wark Griffith, are truncated adaptations and little more than filmed theatrical performances. One of the exceptions is the *Hamlet* filmed by Sir Johnston Forbes-Robertson and Cecil Hepworth in 1913. There are a few successful German films from the 1920s, specifically Hans Neumann's ribald and burlesque rendering of *A Midsummer Night's Dream* in 1925.

The advent of the 'talkies' made Hollywood supreme, bringing Max Reinhardt and William Dieterle's *A Midsummer Night's Dream* (1935) – in which thoroughly kitsch effects (the dance of the fairies in lace and tutus) appear side by side with disturbing hallucinations – and also George Cukor's *Romeo and Juliet* (1936). After the war Marlon Brando distinguished himself in Joseph Mankiewicz's *Julius Caesar* (1953), playing the part of Mark Antony. However, the *Antony and Cleopatra* by the same director, starring Elizabeth Taylor as Cleopatra, is a pasteboard spectacular in glorious technicolor that is best forgotten.

The first major successes came from Britain with the films of Laurence Olivier: *Henry V*, filmed during the Second World War, in 1944, ringing with patriotism, and plunging us back into the Globe Theatre, reconstructed for the opening and closing scenes; *Hamlet* (1948), radically cut, without Rosencrantz or Guildenstern or Fortinbras, in which the prince is

Hans Neumann's 1925 production of *A Midsummer Night's Dream.*

represented from the outset as a young man unable to make up his mind. These films were followed by two others, *Richard III,* filmed in 1955, and *Othello* in 1965, with Olivier in the title role, made up as a superb Ethiopian with an ebony skin.

Orson Welles followed in his footsteps with *Macbeth,* filmed in 1948, *Othello* in 1952 and *Chimes at Midnight* in 1965, a digest consisting of scenes from *Richard II, Henry IV, Part 1* and *Part 2, The Merry Wives of Windsor* and *Henry V.* This is probably the most successful of the three films, communicating a great affection for the character of Falstaff, with whom Orson Welles identified.

Two Italian producers, Renato Castellani and Franco Zeffirelli, filmed English actors in the actual locations of the plays – Verona for *Romeo and Juliet* (Castellani, 1954; Zeffirelli, 1968), Padua for *The Taming of the Shrew* (Zeffirelli, 1967). The film of this play starring Elizabeth Taylor and Richard Burton was enormously successful, as was *Romeo and Juliet* made the following year. Zeffirelli's choice of very young actors for the latter film enabled him to portray with a mixture of charm and passion the romantic cult of adolescent love destroyed by the incomprehension of parents.

Screen adaptations of Shakespeare in the post-war period were marked by the forceful contributions of Russian and Japanese film directors. Grigori Kosintsev, first of all, with a superb *Hamlet* in 1964, followed by *King Lear* in 1970: two films that were acclaimed as masterpieces by critics. Equally gripping and uncontestably even more original are the films of the Japanese Akira Kurosawa. The first, made in 1957, is called *The Throne of Blood* – a brilliantly constructed film that transposes *Macbeth* to the medieval Japan of the Samurai. By comparison Roman Polanski's *Macbeth*, filmed in 1971, seems much less subtle, though it holds a certain fascination with its powerful imagery, mingling realism and fantastic effects. Kurosawa returned to Shakespeare in 1985 with *Ran*, which transposes *King Lear* to the heart of clan warfare, and enacts the tragedy of the old king in a world of declining feudalism, with ferocious battle scenes organized like a ballet in dazzling colours.

Other recent films show that Shakespeare continues to inspire film directors, yielding adaptations that demonstrate as much originality as talent. The young English actor Kenneth Branagh, who played the part of Henry V in Stratford and London before starting his own theatre company, the Renaissance Theatre Company, brought Shakespeare's play *Henry V* to the screen in 1990. He cast

himself in the role of the young king, next to actors such as Derek Jacobi, playing the Chorus, and Judi Dench, as the Hostess. This film, which deliberately takes a different direction to that of Laurence Olivier, seems equally well realized. It has been highly successful in England, the United States and France. In 1991 Franco Zeffirelli tried his hand at tragedy, filming *Hamlet* in various Scottish castles, with the Australian actor Mel Gibson in the role of the prince. The same year Peter Greenaway, the British director of *The Draughtsman's Contract*, directed an adaptation of *The Tempest* called *Prospero's Books*, an elaborate and densely packed spectacle, visually very successful. Sir John Gielgud, with the experience of his eighty-three years, plays an excellent Prospero and also

John Gielgud in *Prospero's Books* by Peter Greenaway, 1991.

lends his voice, modulated and transformed by computer, to all the other characters in the plot. In this film Prospero is the supreme manipulator: the play he writes under our eyes (he is also Shakespeare) incarnates and exorcises all his phantoms.

François Laroque

Shakespeare films

Antony and Cleopatra:
— *Cleopatra*, French film by Henry Andréani, 1910
—*Antony and Cleopatra*, American film by Joseph L. Mankiewicz, with Elizabeth Taylor as Cleopatra and Richard Burton as Mark Antony, 1972
As You Like It:
— English film by Paul Czinner, with Laurence Olivier as Orlando, 1936
Hamlet:
— French film by Clément Maurice, with Sarah Bernhardt in the leading role, 1900
— French film by Georges Méliès, 1907
— English film by E. Hay Plumb, 1913
— English film by Laurence Olivier, 1948
— *Ophelia*, by Claude Chabrol, 1962
— Russian film by Grigori Kosintsev, 1964
— English film by Tony Richardson, 1969
— Italian film by Franco Zeffirelli, 1991
Henry IV, Parts 1 and 2:
— *Chimes at Midnight*, Spanish-Swiss film by Orson Welles, 1965
Henry V:
— English film by Laurence Oliver, with Laurence Olivier in the leading role, 1944
— English film by Kenneth Branagh, with Kenneth Branagh in the leading role, 1990
Julius Caesar:
— *The Death of Julius Caesar*, by Georges Méliès, 1907
— American film by David Bradley, with Charlton Heston in the part of Mark Antony, 1950
— American film by Joseph L. Mankiewicz, with Marlon Brando in the role of Mark Antony, 1953
— English film by Stuart Burge, with Charlton Heston in the part of Mark Antony and John Gielgud in the part of Caesar, 1969
King Lear:
— Russian film by Grigori Kosintsev, 1970

— Danish film by Peter Brook, with Paul Scofield in the title role, 1971
Macbeth:
— French film by André Calmettes, 1910
— American film by Orson Welles, 1948
— *The Throne of Blood,* Japanese film by Akira Kurosawa, 1957
— English film by George Schaefer, 1960
— English film by Roman Polanski, 1971
The Merchant of Venice:
— *Shylock,* French film by Henri Desfontaines, with Harry Baur in the part of Shylock, 1913
— film by Peter Paul Felner, 1923
The Merry Wives of Windsor:
— German film by Georg Wildhagen, 1950
A Midsummer Night's Dream:
— American film by Max Reinhardt and William Dieterle, with James Cagney in the part of Bottom, 1935
— English film by Peter Hall, 1969
Othello:
— German film with Emil Jannings in the part of Othello and Werner Krauss in that of Iago, 1922
— American film by Orson Welles with Orson Welles in the leading role, 1952
— Russian film by Sergei Yutkevitch, 1955
— English film by Stuart Burge, with Laurence Olivier in the leading role, 1965
Richard III:
— English film by Laurence Olivier, 1955
Romeo and Juliet:
— American film by George Cukor, with Norma Shearer in the role of Juliet and Leslie Howard in that of Romeo, 1936
— *The Lovers of Verona*, French film by André Cayatte and Jacques Prévert, 1949
—Italian and English film by Renato Castellani, 1954
—Italian and English film by Franco Zeffirelli, 1968
The Taming of the Shrew:
— French film by Henri Desfontaines, 1911
— Italian film by Franco Zeffirelli, with Richard Burton and Elizabeth Taylor, 1967
The Tempest:
— English film by Derek Jarman, 1980
— English film by Paul Mazursky, 1982
— *Prospero's Books*, English film by Peter Greenaway, 1991
Twelfth Night:
— Russian film by Yan Fried, 1955
The Winter's Tale:
— English film by Frank Dunlop, 1966

The Shakespeare industry

Every year some five thousand works about Shakespeare are published. Indeed, since the end of the Second World War a virtual industry has developed, producing books, theses and articles on the playwright. Originating in American universities, it has now spread throughout Europe.

Writing about Shakespeare far exceeds anything available on any other English or American writer. Despite the great range of bibliographies, concordances, syntheses, summaries and abstracts, it is difficult to keep up to date. The proliferation of critical material is, indeed, enough to discourage any student or scholar from embarking on the study of Shakespeare. Yet the craze shows no sign of abating in English- and German-speaking countries, where Shakespeare studies continue their relentless advance. In France and other Latin countries, where the reputedly difficult language of the plays is an obstacle, the situation is different. But new translations and editions,

The Royal Shakespeare Theatre, Stratford.

combined with the success of recent adaptations for stage and cinema, are likely to stimulate the still somewhat tentative French interest in Shakespeare.

The activities of the universities are matched by those of the theatres and actors. In Stratford-upon-Avon there are three permanent theatres: the Royal Shakespeare Theatre (RST), originally built in 1879 thanks to the generosity of Charles Edward Flower, a rich brewer of the region, and rebuilt after a fire in 1933; the little theatre known as The Other Place, formerly used for rehearsals, which opened to the public in 1974 and was recently rebuilt to meet present-day safety standards; and the Swan Theatre, a wooden structure copied from the private theatres of the 17th century and adjoining the Royal

Shakespeare Theatre. It opened its doors in 1986. The season lasts virtually the whole year (beginning in April with the official celebration of Shakespeare's birthday and finishing at the end of January) and runs concurrently with the same company's season at the Barbican Theatre, London. In the course of it some fifteen plays are performed, the most successful of which are put on at the Barbican Theatre in London. In addition to these theatres there are the National Theatre, founded just before Shakespeare's quadricentenary, and for a long time managed by Sir Laurence Olivier, the Young Vic, the Aldwych and the open-air theatre in Regent's Park, all of which feature Shakespeare's plays prominently.

Outside the Royal Shakespeare Company, new companies have been established in recent years, despite the severe financial pressures affecting the British performing arts after public

Shakespeare's birthplace as it was in 1769 (top), and 1851 (centre) and as it is today.

subsidies were reduced under Margaret Thatcher. These include the English Shakespeare Company managed by Michael Bogdanov, and the Renaissance Theatre managed by Kenneth Branagh, both with noteworthy productions to their credit. The plan to build a new Globe Theatre next to Shakespeare's theatre, the foundations of which have recently been discovered, should soon become reality now that all the legal and financial obstacles to its construction have been removed. This is largely thanks to the efforts of Sam Wanamaker, an actor who has devoted a considerable amount of time and energy to realizing the project.

In the summer visitors come in large numbers from the four corners of the world to see the plays billed in the three Stratford theatres and to visit the town of Shakespeare's birth. The Japanese are particularly interested in this shrine of western culture. It was in fact in the Japanese capital Tokyo that the 1991 world congress on Shakespeare took place, bringing together nearly a thousand delegates.

Shakespeare studies in their current dynamic state depend on a number of institutions. First of all there are the large specialized libraries: those of the Shakespeare Centre and the Shakespeare Institute at Stratford-upon-Avon, the Folger Shakespeare Library in Washington D.C., and the Huntington Library at San Marino in California. Research in the form of articles, reports and bibliographies is published and circulated in various periodicals. The oldest of these is *Shakespeare Jahrbuch*, founded in 1865 in Berlin; the most prestigious, *Shakespeare Survey*, is published in

THE SWAN
THEATRE

The Swan Theatre, Stratford.

Cambridge, England; the principal American publications are the *Shakespeare Quarterly*, launched in New York in 1950 and handed over to the Folger Library in 1972, and *Shakespeare Studies*, founded in Cincinnati in 1965. In France the review *Cahiers Elisabéthains* (Elizabethan Notebooks), founded in 1972 at the Université Paul-Valéry of Montpellier, publishes some French and foreign research on Shakespeare and the Elizabethan period in its twice-yearly issues.

Most major countries have a society for Shakespeare studies. The oldest is the 'Deutsche Shakespeare Gesellschaft', founded in Weimar in 1865. The more recent French Shakespeare Society dates from 1975. One of the most active societies outside the United States, where there are a great many 'Shakespeareans', is the Shakespeare Society of Japan, now numbering eight hundred members. This is clear evidence of the popularity of the playwright's work in the Land of the Rising Sun. All these national societies belong to the International Shakespeare Association, founded in 1972, which organizes a world congress every four years. The first was held at Vancouver, the most recent in Tokyo. But Stratford remains the Mecca for Shakespeare studies, and it is there that the week-long Shakespeare Conference is held in August every two years, bringing together in the Shakespeare Institute all the experts in the work of the great Elizabethan playwright.

François Laroque

FURTHER READING

Complete works of Shakespeare

Brooks, Harold F., Harold Jenkins and Brian Morris (eds), *The Arden Shakespeare*, 1951–

Wells, Stanley, and Gary Taylor (eds), *William Shakespeare, The Complete Works* (The Oxford Shakespeare), 1986–

Shakespeare's life

Bentley, Gerald Eades, *Shakespeare: A Biographical Handbook*, 1961

Bradbrook, Muriel, *Shakespeare. The Poet in His World*, 1978

Brinkworth, E.R.C., *New Light on the Life of Shakespeare*, 1975

Burgess, Anthony, *Shakespeare*, 1970

Chambers, Edmund K., *William Shakespeare, A Study of Facts and Problems*, 2 vols, 1930

– *Sources for a Biography of William Shakespeare*, 1946

Halliday, F.E., *The Life of Shakespeare*, 1961

Levi, Peter, *The Life and Times of William Shakespeare*, 1988

Quennell, Peter, *Shakespeare: The Poet and His Background*, 1963

Rowse, A.L., *William Shakespeare: A Biography*, 1963

– *Shakespeare the Man*, 1973

Schoenbaum, Samuel, *Shakespeare's Lives*, 1970

– *William Shakespeare. A Documentary Life*, 1975

– *William Shakespeare. A Compact Documentary Life*, 1977

Reference and criticism

Armstrong, William A. (ed.), *Shakespeare's Histories*, 1972

Bradby, Anne (ed.), *Shakespeare Criticism, 1919-35*, 1936

Bradley, A.C., *Shakespearean Tragedy*, 1904

Bullough, Geoffrey (ed.), *Narrative and Dramatic Sources of Shakespeare*, 1957

Coleridge, Samuel Taylor, *Shakespearian Criticism*, 2 vols, 1960

Colie, Rosalie, *Shakespeare's Living Art*, 1974

Dyson, A.E., *Casebook Series* (1 vol. per play), 1968–

Empson, William, *Essays on Shakespeare*, 1986

Fluchère, Henri, *Shakespeare Elizabethan Dramatist*, 1947

French, Marilyn, *Shakespeare's Division of Experience*, 1982

Frye, Northrop, *On Shakespeare*, 1986

Granville-Barker, Harley, *Prefaces to Shakespeare*, 2 vols, 1930

Greg, W.W., *The First Folio*, 1953

Halliday, F.E., *A Shakespeare Companion, 1564–1964*, 1964

Kott, Jan, *Shakespeare Our Contemporary*, 1962

Laroque, François, *Shakespeare's Festive World*, 1991

Lerner, Laurence (ed.), *Shakespeare's Tragedies*, 1963

– *Shakespeare's Comedies*, 1967

Muir, Kenneth, *The Sources of Shakespeare's Plays*, 1977

Reese, M.M., *Shakespeare, His World and His Work*, 1953

Righter, Anne, *Shakespeare and the Idea of the Play*, 1962

Rowse, A.L., *Prefaces to Shakespeare's Plays*, 1981

Salinger, Leo, *Shakespeare and the Traditions of Comedy*, 1974

Schücking, L.L., *Character Problems in Shakespeare's Plays*, 1922

Smith, D. Nichol (ed.), *Shakespeare Criticism*, 1916

Spurgeon, Caroline, *Shakespeare's Imagery and What It Tells Us*, 1935

Taylor, Gary, *Reinventing Shakespeare*, 1990

Tillyard, Eustace M.W., *The Elizabethan World Picture*, 1943

Vickers, Brian, *Shakespeare, The Critical Heritage*, 6 vols, 1974–81

Wells, Stanley (ed.), *Shakespeare, An Illustrated Dictionary*, 1978

– *The Cambridge Companion to Shakespeare Studies*, 1986

– *Shakespeare. A Bibliographical Guide*, 1990

Wiles, David, *Shakespeare's Clown*, 1987

Woodhuysen, H.R. (ed.), *Samuel Johnson on Shakespeare*, 1989

Periodicals

Shakespeare Jahrbuch (essays in English and German), from 1865

Shakespeare Survey, from 1948

Shakespeare Quarterly, from 1950

Shakespeare Studies, from 1965

CHRONOLOGY

1564 26 April: baptism of William, third child of John Shakespeare of Snitterfield and Mary Arden of Wilmcote. (Shakespeare's parents came from the vicinity of Stratford, where they married in 1557.)

1568 John Shakespeare becomes bailiff of Stratford. The Queen's Men put on plays in the town

1576 John Shakespeare's fortunes decline

1582 28 November: William Shakespeare marries Anne Hathaway (born 1556)

1583 26 May: baptism of Susanna, born to William and Anne six months after their wedding

1585 2 February: baptism of William and Anne's twins, Hamnet and Judith

1587 The Queen's and Leicester's companies perform in Stratford. William may have returned to London with them

1588 The destruction of the Spanish Armada and Spanish plans to land on the British coast

1590–2 First performances of the historical trilogy *Henry VI*

1592 3 March: Henslowe mentions the performance of *Henry VI* in his diary. Robert Greene's attack on Shakespeare is posthumously published by Henry Chettle (who apologized to Shakespeare in a subsequent work). The plague ravages London, where theatres are closed, with rare intermissions, until May 1594. There are over twenty thousand victims

1596 11 August: Hamnet, Judith's twin brother and Shakespeare's only son, dies aged eleven

1597 Shakespeare buys the house New Place, Stratford, for £60

1598 The first publication of a play under Shakespeare's name: the quarto of *Love's Labour's Lost*. In September Shakespeare acts in Ben Jonson's comedy, *Every Man in His Humour*

1598–9 The Theatre in Shoreditch is taken to pieces by Burbage and rebuilt as the Globe at Southwark, on the other side of the Thames

1601 Performance of *Richard II* at the Globe on 7 February just before Essex's rebellion

1603 The Chamberlain's Men become the King's Men by royal licence. In London, between March 1603 and April 1604, thirty thousand die of the plague. The king's arrival in the city is postponed by a year

1605–9 Another epidemic of the plague in London. 5 November 1605: the Gunpowder Plot led by Guy Fawkes

1607 5 June: Shakespeare's elder daughter Susanna marries John Hall, a well-known doctor in Stratford

1608 Shakespeare is one of the founders of the covered theatre of Blackfriars. On 9 September his mother is buried

1610 Presumed year of Shakespeare's return to Stratford, to his house New Place

1612 3 February: Shakespeare's brother Gilbert is buried. In May Shakespeare testifies in the Belott-Mountjoy suit. The earliest surviving example of his signature is at the end of his deposition. (The others are on his will.)

1613 29 June: the Globe burns down

1616 10 February: at Stratford Shakespeare's younger daughter Judith marries Thomas Quiney, son of a family friend. 25 March: Shakespeare signs his will. 23 April: (probably his fifty-second birthday) Shakespeare dies and is buried two days later, on 25 April

1623 Death of Shakespeare's widow Anne. Publication of the First Folio, the first edition of his complete plays (only *Pericles* and *The Two Noble Kinsmen* are missing)

SHAKESPEARE'S WORKS

The plays

1589–90	*Henry VI, Part 1*
1590–1	*Henry VI, Part 2, Henry VI, Part 3*
1592–3	*Richard III, Titus Andronicus*
1593–4	*The Comedy of Errors, The Taming of the Shrew*
1594–5	*The Two Gentlemen of Verona, Love's Labour's Lost*
1595–6	*Romeo and Juliet, Richard II, A Midsummer Night's Dream*
1596–7	*King John, The Merchant of Venice*
1597–8	*Henry IV, Part 1, Henry IV, Part 2*
1598–9	*Much Ado About Nothing, Henry V, The Merry Wives of Windsor*
1599–1600	*Julius Caesar, As You Like It, Twelfth Night*
1600–01	*Hamlet*
1601–2	*Troilus and Cressida*

1602–3	*All's Well That Ends Well, Othello*
1603	*Measure for Measure*
1604–5	*King Lear*
1605–6	*Macbeth*
1606–7	*Antony and Cleopatra, Timon of Athens*
1607–8	*Coriolanus*
1608–9	*Pericles*
1609–10	*Cymbeline*
1610–11	*The Winter's Tale*
1611–2	*The Tempest*
1612–3	*Henry VIII*
1613–4	*The Two Noble Kinsmen*

The poems

1593	*Venus and Adonis*
1594	*The Rape of Lucrece*
1609	*The Sonnets*

LIST OF ILLUSTRATIONS

The following abbreviations have been used: *a* above, *b* below, *c* centre, *l* left, *r* right;. BL British Library, London, BM Department of Prints and Drawings, British Museum, London, Bod Lib Bodleian Library, Oxford, NPG National Portrait Gallery, London, V&A Victoria and Albert Museum, London.

COVER

OPENING

CHAPTER 1

CHAPTER 2

CHAPTER 3

CHAPTER 4

CHAPTER 5

DOCUMENTS

INDEX

Figures in *italic* refer to pages on which captions appear.

PHOTO CREDITS

All Rights Reserved 12, 13, 15, 17 *br*, 18–9 *b*, 20, 21 *c*, 21 *b*, 22, 24–5 *c*, 24–5 *b*, 36–7, 37 *al* and *br*, 38 *l*, 38 *br*, 39 *ar*, 39 *l*, 44–5 *b*, 48 *b*, 49, 52 *a*, 54 *b*, 56 *a*, 57 *a*, 59 *a*, 63 *ar*, 64–5 *b*, 65 *a*, 70, 71 *a*, 84 *c*, 88, 89 *a*, 98–9 *b*, 100 *a*, 101 *b*, 103 *a*, 103 *br*, 104 *a*, 104 *b*, 106–7 *a*, 107 *b*, 114 *b*, 116–7 *b*, 119 *al*, 119 *ar*, 129, 170, 180–1; Ashmolean Museum, Oxford 73 *al*, 107 *ar*; Marquess of Bath 56–7 *b*; Bodleian Library, Oxford back cover, 27 *b*, 76 *a*, 84 *a*, 108; Bridgeman Art Library 14, 18–9 *c*, 21 *a*, 40, 44–5 *a*, 90, 91, 92–3, 101 *a*, 109, 110–1 *a*, 126, 151; British Film Institute, London 174 *b*, 177; British Library, London front cover, spine, 1, 23 *a*, 23 *b*, 29 *b*, 37 *ar*, 42–3 *b*, 43 *a*, 52–3 *b*, 75 *ar*, 76 *b*, 82, 85 *ar*, 85 *b*, 89 *b*, 105, 110–1 *b*, 116–7 *a*, 120, 143, 144, 145; British Museum, London front cover, 46 *c*, 46–7 *b*, 60, 113 *a*; Duke of Buccleuch and Queensberry KT 58 *a*; Cahiers du Cinéma 178; Trustees of the Chatsworth Settlement 115 *l*, 115 *r*; Christie's Colour Library, London 34–5 *b*; College of Arms, London 58–9 *b*; Donald Cooper 174 *a*; Corpus Christi College, Cambridge 50; Viscount De L'Isle MBE, Penshurst Place 98–9 *a*; Dulwich College 55 *c*, 69 *b*; Dulwich Picture Gallery 73 *ac*, 73 *ar*, 83 *a*; Edinburgh University Library 2–3, 4–5, 6–7, 8–9, 47 *a*, 54–5 *a*, 66–7, 110 *c*, 112–3 *b*; E.T. Archive 18–9 *a*, 64 *a*, 72 *a*, 74–5, 92 *al*, 93 *ar*, 120–1, 122–3, 124–5; Fitzwilliam Museum, Cambridge 24–5 *a*; Folger Shakespeare Library, Washington, D.C. 26, 28–9 *a*, 57 *c*, 87 *ar*; Fotomas 16–7 *c*, 34–5 *a*, 94 *br*; A. Fulgoni 139; Greater London Record Office 62 *bl*; Guildhall Library, London 65 *a*, 132; Louisa Hare 48 *a*, 52 *b*, 53 *a*, 71 *b*, 83 *b*, 85 *al*, 112 *a*, 118 *a* and *b*, 119 *cr*; Ipswich Museums and Galleries 77, 78, 79, 80, 81 *a*, 81 *b*; lefevre Gallery, London 169; Museum of London 69 *a*; National Gallery, London 102–3 *a*; National Portrait Gallery, London 11, 32–3, 51, 94 *ar*, 94 *bl*, 95, 102–3 *a*, 114 *a*, 116 *al*; Private collections 54 *a*, 102 *b*, 103 *bl*; Public Record Office, London 126–7, 135; Rein, Stiftsarchiv 72–3 *b*; Royal Armouries 99 *c*; Royal Collection, courtesy of Her Majesty the Queen 96–7, 106; Royal Shakespeare Company 180–1, 183; Royal Shakespeare Theatre Collection, Stratford-upon-Avon 86; Scala 94 *al*; Shakespeare Birthplace Trust, Stratford-upon-Avon 16–7 *a*, 87 *al*, 87 *b*, 149, 170, 171, 172; Shakespeare Institute, University of Birmingham 61; Edwin Smith 182 *b*; Society of Antiquaries, London 41; Tate Gallery, London 165; Eileen Tweedy 158; Utrecht, Bibliothek der Rijksuniversiteit 62 *a*, 68.

ACKNOWLEDGMENTS

The author thanks Suzanne Bosman in London, Susan Brock, Stanley Wells, Director of the Shakespeare Institute in Birmingham, Christian Biet, Bernard Tannier, and the Centre d'études et de recherches élisabéthaines of the Université Paul-Valéry at Montpellier.

Grateful acknowledgment is made for permission to use material from the following works: (p. 168) *The Woman's Part* by Carolyn Ruth Swift Lenz, Gayle Greene and Carol Thomas Neely, Copyright © 1980 by Carolyn Ruth Swift Lenz, Gayle Greene and Carol Thomas Neely; (pp. 165–6) *Reinventing Shakespeare* by Gary Taylor, © 1989 by Gary Taylor; (pp.166–7) *Shakespeare Our Contemporary* by Jan Kott, © 1964, Pánstwowe Wydawnictwo Naukowe (PWN Polish Scientific Publishers), Warszawa; (p. 169) *Shakespeare's Division of Experience* by Marilyn French, © 1981, Marilyn French

François Laroque
teaches English literature
at the university of the Sorbonne nouvelle, Paris III.
He is a Shakespeare specialist and is a member of the
Centre d'études et de recherches élisabéthaines at the
Université Paul-Valéry in Montpellier.
He has written numerous articles on Shakespeare's
plays and on the attitudes and folklore
of Elizabethan England. He is the author of
Shakespeare et la fête (1988) and has also collaborated
on an anthology of English literature (1991).

© 1991 Gallimard
English translation © Thames and Hudson Ltd,
London, and Harry N. Abrams, Inc., New York,
1993

Translated by Alexandra Campbell

British Library Cataloguing-in-Publication Data

A catalogue record for this book is available from the
British Library

ISBN 0-500-30035-6

Printed and bound in Italy
by Editoriale Libraria, Trieste